LED-ZEPPELIN

 W9-CMS-906

MOTHERSHIP

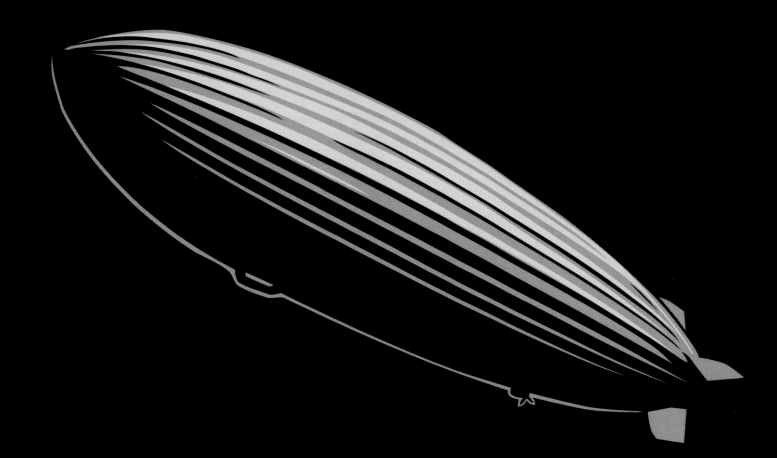

Photography: CHRISTIAN ROSE/DALLE/IDOLS

Foreword: DAVID FRICKE

 Alfred

Alfred Publishing Co., Inc.
16320 Roscoe Blvd., Suite 100
P.O. Box 10003
Van Nuys, CA 91410-0003
alfred.com

ISBN-10: 0-7390-5317-5
ISBN-13: 978-0-7390-5317-1

"HOT, NEW ENGLISH GROUP LED ZEPPELIN"

It was a modest announcement, a two-page press release issued in November 1968: "Atlantic Records has signed the hot, new English group Led Zeppelin to a long-term exclusive recording contract. Although the exact terms of the deal are secret, it can be disclosed that it is one of most substantial deals Atlantic has ever made."

Most of what followed was quick biography—Jimmy Page's history with The Yardbirds, where he had succeeded Eric Clapton and Jeff Beck as lead guitarist, and as one of the best and busiest session musicians in Britain; bassist John Paul Jones' success as an arranger of hit records for Donovan and The Rolling Stones, among many others. There were references to drummer John Bonham's already notorious solos as a member of American singer Tim Rose's touring band and to Robert Plant's blooming reputation as "one of England's outstanding young blues singers."

There was a promise too. "Top English and American rock musicians who have heard the tracks," the release said, referring to Zeppelin's imminent debut album, "have compared the LP to the best of Cream and Jimi Hendrix and have called Led Zeppelin the next group to reach the heights achieved by Cream and Hendrix."

That was audacious talk, a fat power chord in the face, at a time when Hendrix still walked the Earth and Cream were a fresh memory—the latter played their farewell shows that very month at London's Royal Albert Hall. In comparison, when Led Zeppelin opened their first North American tour in Denver, Colorado, on December 26, 1968, they were third on a bill to Vanilla Fudge and Spirit and treated like a doormat. The promoter, Plant told me years later, deducted the cost of the backstage grub—"this four-loaves-and-five-fishes thing"—from the band's pay. At other dates, Plant operated Zeppelin's P.A. system himself, onstage, and Bonham often played without miking his kit (a minor annoyance as he was loud enough

without electricity). In Detroit a local newspaper ad for Zeppelin's three-night stand at the Grande Ballroom announced the appearance of "Led Zeptlin."

But as Page said later, recalling that tour, "You could feel something happening—first this row, then that row. It was like a tornado, and it went rolling across the country." By the end of 1969, Page, Plant, Jones, and Bonham had torn through North America four times, each time to bigger, sold-out audiences. In Britain, where they had been in clubs as The New Yardbirds as late as October 1968, Zeppelin quickly followed Cream into the Royal Albert Hall, filling it in June 1969 (and again in January 1970). In that first whiplash year, Led Zeppelin also released two of the most exciting and important rock albums ever made, *Led Zeppelin* and *Led Zeppelin II*—together, the fundamental bones of hard rock and heavy metal for the next four decades.

From the start, Led Zeppelin were working warriors. They toured like dogs—albeit in wild-boy luxury, fiercely protected by their manager, Peter Grant—and made eight studio albums (one a double LP) at a pace that now seems superhuman. Page claimed the total recording time for *Led Zeppelin* was 30 hours. The band made *II* on rare off days between shows in the summer of '69, in nearly a dozen different studios. "I remember we did vocal overdubs in an eight-track studio in Vancouver where they didn't even have proper headphones," Page recalled in a 1977 interview with Dave Schulps for the American magazine *Trans-Oceanic Trouser Press.* "Can you imagine that?"

Actually, yes. Even the band's harshest critics—and there were armies of them at the time—could not deny that Led Zeppelin had a rare drive to excel and conquer. "So many people are frightened to take a chance in life," Page told *Rolling Stone's* Cameron Crowe in 1975, "and there's so many chances you have to take." Jones did not hesitate to give up the regular,

lucrative checks from his studio gigs to be in Led Zeppelin; as soon as he heard about Page's plans for a new group, in the late summer of '68, he called Page and *asked* to join. Page himself was throwing dice when, on the recommendation of Terry Reid (who turned down Page's offer to be vocalist), he checked out and hired Plant, just 20 and unknown beyond the club grind in England's industrial Midlands. Page then took Plant's advice and grabbed the singer's friend, Bonham.

"It was a series of intense, dynamic crescendos, one right after the other," Plant told me, describing Zeppelin's first American shows in 1968 and '69. "There was no room for the letdown." That is also a perfect description of the power, confidence, and desire—the lust for liftoff—in these songs and performances. Led Zeppelin wanted everything, in record time. And they were afraid of nothing. *Mothership*—the peak of their canon—is what No Fear sounds like.

The first four songs here, all from *Led Zeppelin*, are the work of a new band racing against clock and budget to connect their individual histories and collective passions into a new, huge music. The roots are unmistakeable, the combination unprecedented: the blues, twang, and holler of America's Deep South and black urban neighborhoods, especially anything bearing the classic Chess, Sun, and Atlantic labels; the British folk renaissance; California Day-Glo psychedelia.

So are the ambitions. "Good Times Bad Times" and "Communication Breakdown" are as tightly arranged as any candy-pop 45 Page and Jones played on as hired guns. But the details are explosive: Bonham's avalanche rolls and Jones' pummeling bass outbursts in "Good Times Bad Times"; the nuclear buckshot of Page's chords behind Plant's arcing wail in "Communication Breakdown," which takes off like a fuzz-rocket son of The Yardbirds' "Train Kept A-Rollin'" and still feels way too short at two minutes and change. "Babe I'm Gonna Leave You" was a folk ballad Page knew from Joan Baez's recording on her 1962 album, *Joan Baez In Concert.* But there was nothing purist or polite about his *Led Zeppelin* arrangement: the echo-soaked mass of acoustic and electric guitars; Plant's white heat in the double-time break.

"I had a long ways to go with my voice then," Plant admitted to Crowe. "But at the same time, the enthusiasm and spark of working with Jimmy's guitar shows through quite well"—a telepathy imprinted in "Dazed And Confused," a song Page brought to Zeppelin from The Yardbirds' last tours. Here, Jones carries the riff, with Page's low-growl and soprano-fuzz guitars lined up behind him. But Plant and Page soon leap out front like warring twins: Plant mimicking Page's bowed-guitar moans; the two shrieking in tandem over Bonham and Jones' racing precision. Page and Plant's harmonized cries and call-response theater were as old as plantation field hollers and country-church hosannas. They were also a special, crucial excitement on Led Zeppelin's records, and you get it here, repeatedly, in a variety of settings: the immortal start of *Led Zeppelin II,* as Plant flies and dives through Page's guitar violence in the hurricane center of "Whole Lotta Love"; Plant's Viking yell against Page's rusted gallop in "Immigrant Song" on *Led Zeppelin III;* the searing vocal-guitar mantra, suspended in Himalayan-blizzard phasing, in "Nobody's Fault But Mine" on the 1976 album *Presence;* the sundown-prayer call of "In The Evening" on 1979's *In Through The Out Door.*

Page was modest when he talked about his guitar prowess with Crowe in 1975: "I'm not a guitarist as far as a technician goes—I just pick it up and play it. Technique doesn't come into it. I deal in emotions." That explains his crazed, slashing outbursts in "Whole Lotta Love" and "Heartbreaker" on II and the raw convulsion of his breaks in the slow blues "Since I've Been Loving You" on *III.* That last track was cut live in the studio—note the dark magic of Jones' Hammond-organ bed—and Page later dismissed his soloing: "It could have been better." Yet that

spontaneous fury reflected Page's stubborn faith in the power of "spontaneous combustion," as he once described the creation of the Little Richard-style dragster "Rock And Roll," even as Zeppelin's records became more eclectic and complex.

Page took no chances on Led Zeppelin's officially untitled fourth album (usually called *IV* or *Zoso* after one of the runes, representing each band member, on the inner sleeve). He spent nearly as much time mixing the eight tracks as the band did recording them, delaying the album's release for half a year. "When The Levee Breaks"—adapted by Zeppelin from a blues recorded by Kansas Joe McCoy and Memphis Minnie about the catastrophic Mississippi River flood of 1927—"is probably the most subtle thing on there," Page said in the *Trouser Press* interview. "Each twelve bars has something new about it . . . phased vocals, a backwards-echoed harmonica solo"—all nailed to your skull by one of the heaviest and, in the hip-hop age, most sampled drumbeats in rock.

"I don't want to sound that dictatorial, though," he insisted, "because it's not that sort of thing at all. When we went into Headley Grange [an old almshouse in East Hampshire, England, where most of *IV* was recorded], it was more like 'Okay, what's anybody got?'" Jones, for example, had the volcanic-bebop riff that became "Black Dog."

Ironically, *IV*'s crowning track, "Stairway To Heaven," is so popular (to the point of backlash—you can get thrown out of guitar stores for playing the opening lick) that it is easy to miss why the song "crystallized the essence of the band," as Page said in 1975. "It had everything there and showed the band at its best—as a band, as a unit."

"It was a very successful song," Jones affirmed later, "successful in that everything worked well and fell into place."

"Stairway To Heaven" is a masterpiece of heavy rock 'n' roll scoring with a surprising moral center. (The opening lines, Plant said, were "a cynical aside about a woman getting everything she wanted all the time without giving back any thought or consideration.") The music literally ascends in distinct, melodic episodes, from the magnetic quiet of Page's classic arpeggio and Jones' haunted recorder to the sudden shine of those 12-string chords and the total victory of Page's final solo. There may be no higher compliment to his perfectly articulated dynamite at the end of "Stairway To Heaven" than the cover version I saw Frank Zappa play at a New York show in 1988, complete with a ten-piece horn section that followed Page's solo note for note, in carefully scored harmony—a dramatic bow of respect from one guitar master to another.

With *IV,* Led Zeppelin's ascent was complete. There would be no bigger band in the '70s, in ticket sales (Zeppelin were filling U.S. football stadiums before The Rolling Stones), record sales (every album here went Top 10 in *Billboard*; all but two went to #1), and in off-stage excess (well-documented elsewhere). But restless adventuring had been an early theme in Plant's writing—in the Middle Earth geography of "Ramble On" on *II* and the snapshots of midnight sun and hot springs in "Immigrant Song," written after Zeppelin played in Reykjavik, Iceland, in June 1970.

To Plant, the essence and promise of Led Zeppelin was in "the quest, the travels and explorations that Page and I went on to far climes well off the beaten track," he told me in a 1988 interview. World domination obviously had its benefits. "I had a dream/Crazy dream/Anything I wanted to know, any place I needed to go," Plant crowed in "The Song Remains The Same" on 1973's *Houses Of The Holy*. Except it was no dream. By then, Bron-Yr-Aur, a remote cottage in southern Wales, was famous for the songs Page and Plant wrote there in 1970 and '71; Page and Plant had also recorded in India with members of the Bombay Symphony. "D'yer

Mak'er" may have been tongue-in-cheek reggae (say the title real fast), but the blunt-instrument treble of Jones' bass was authentic homage to the truly heavy bottom and primitive fidelity of Jamaican records and rhythm sections. (Page often put Jones way up in Zeppelin mixes; in "Houses Of The Holy," originally cut for that album, the chugging bass is louder and dirtier than Page's guitar.)

"Of course, we only touched the surface," Plant said of those excursions with Page between records and tours. "We weren't anthropologists. But we were allowed, because we were musicians, to be invited in societies that people don't normally witness. It was quite a remarkable time, to open your eyes and see how Berber tribesmen lived in the northern Sahara"—a memorable trip that inspired the thundering march and orchestral sandstorm of "Kashmir" on the 1975 double album *Physical Graffiti*.

Jones' skills as an orchestrator and multi-instrumentalist, rarely mentioned even in rave reviews of the band's records, were pivotal in Zeppelin's songs of pilgrimage (real and imagined). The mounting doom of "No Quarter" on *Houses Of The Holy* starts with the simple, compelling black-liquid ripple of his electric piano. In "Kashmir" staccato strings march alongside Page's climbing guitar, and long mellotron chords roll over the horizon like clouds of dust. When I asked Plant, in 1988, about "Stairway To Heaven" and its status as the definitive Zeppelin song, he immediately corrected me. "It's not," he said. "'Kashmir' is."

Ultimately, everything here is definitive Zeppelin, in some way: the rude, thundering funk of "Trampled Under Foot," driven by Jones' percolating clavinet and Bonham's merciless drumming; the ferocious, prolonged assault of "Achilles Last Stand" (Page told Dave Schulps that he meticulously orchestrated the song's horde of guitars "in my mind," then recorded "all the overdubs in one night"); and the elegant sweep and memorial tenderness of "All My Love."

Then, suddenly, there was no Zeppelin. On September 25, 1980, a day after the group convened to rehearse for yet another North American tour, Bonham was found dead at Page's home, following a mammoth drinking binge. "The band didn't exist," Plant said later, "the minute Bonzo died."

The music and history were left unfinished. On December 4 Atlantic Records issued a one-sentence press release: "We wish it to be known that the loss of our dear friend and the deep respect we have for his family, together with the sense of undivided harmony felt by ourselves and our manager, have led us to decide that we could not continue as we were." It was simply signed "Led Zeppelin."

The end came with ironic timing— 12 years almost to the day after Atlantic sent out that first announcement in 1968. It also sealed the purity and power of everything Jimmy Page, Robert Plant, John Paul Jones, and John Bonham wrote and played together in what now seems like a very short time. Led Zeppelin did not last long enough to fail. Instead, they have a unique, eternal life in this music that can never be tainted and will never be topped.

The band is gone. The thrill is not.

—David Fricke

LED·ZEPPELIN·MOTHERSHIP
CONTENTS

LED·ZEPPELIN·MOTHERSHIP

GOOD TIMES BAD TIMES

Words and Music by
JIMMY PAGE, JOHN PAUL JONES
and JOHN BONHAM

*Elec. Gtr. 1 is very faint in the mix.

In the days of my youth, I was told _ what it means _ to be a man. _

*Let ring

*Let arpeggiated figures ring
throughout unless notated otherwise.

Good Times Bad Times - 10 - 1

mat-ter how I try,_ I find my way in - to the same_ old_ jam._

end Rhy. Fig. 1

Chorus:

Good times, bad _ times,_ you know I've had _ my share._ Well, my

Let ring   *Let ring*   *Rush tempo*

wom-an left home for a brown-eyed man, __ but I still don't seem to care. _____

Six - teen I fell __ in love _____ with a girl as sweet as could be. __ It

Elec. Gtrs. 1 & 2

on - ly took a cou - ple of days __ 'til she was rid of me. __ She

*Parenthesised notes played by
Elec. Gtr. 1 only*

Chorus:

swore that she would be ___ all mine and love me 'til the end, ___

when I whis-pered in her ear ___ I lost an-oth-er friend. ___ Oh!

Good times, bad times, ___ you know I've had my share. ___ Well, my

Elec. Gtr. 1

Elec. Gtr. 2

Let ring   Let ring

wom-an left home for a brown-eyed man, __ but I still don't seem to care. __

Guitar Solo:
w/Fill 1 *(Elec. Gtr. 3) 8 times*

Fill 1
Elec. Gtr. 3

Even gliss.

COMMUNICATION BREAKDOWN

Words and Music by
JIMMY PAGE, JOHN PAUL JONES
and JOHN BONHAM

Fast rock ♩ = 174

Intro:

Verse 1:

Hey, girl, stop what you're do-in'.

Rhy. Fig. 1

end Rhy. Fig. 1

Chorus:

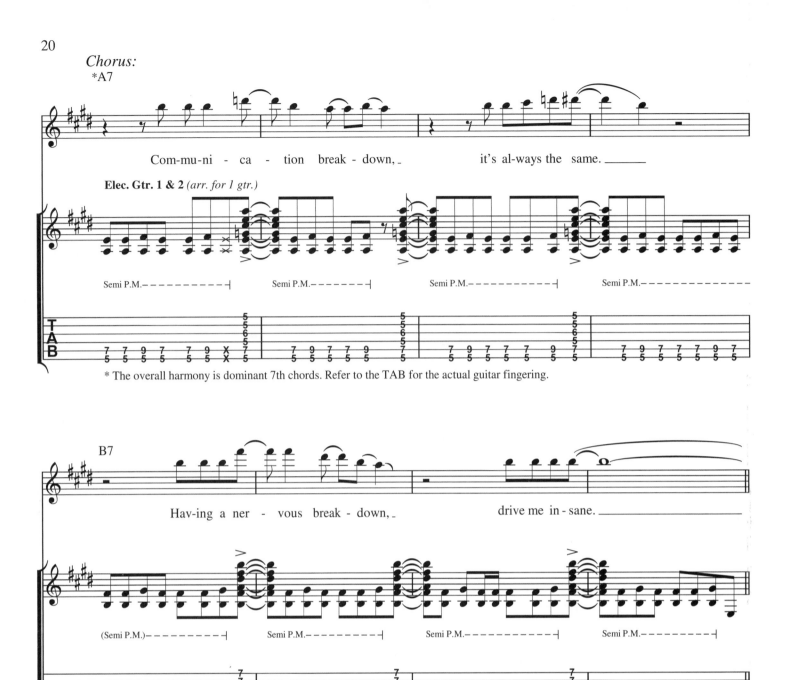

* The overall harmony is dominant 7th chords. Refer to the TAB for the actual guitar fingering.

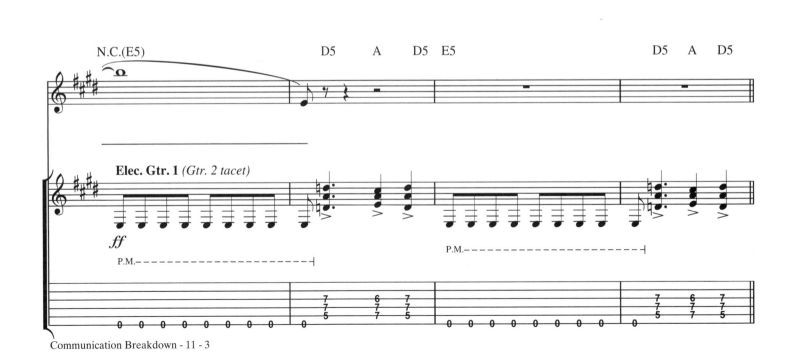

Verse 2:

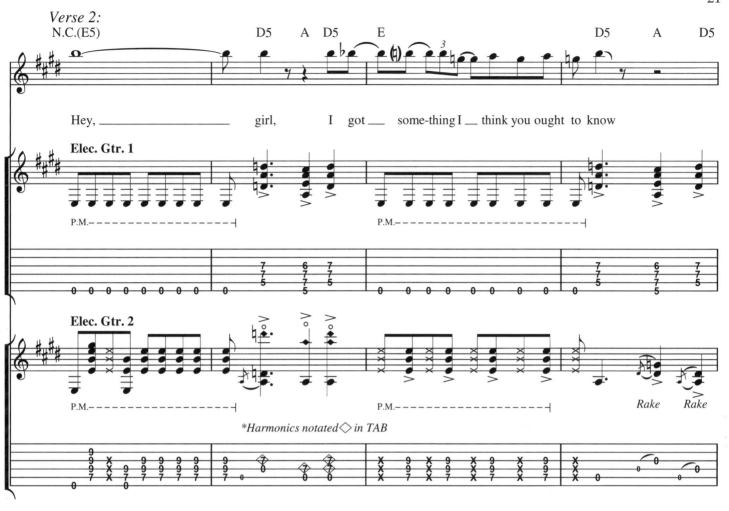

Hey, _____ girl, I got ___ some-thing I __ think you ought to know

*Harmonics notated ◇ in TAB

Hey, ____ babe, __ I wan-na tell you that I ____ love you so. __

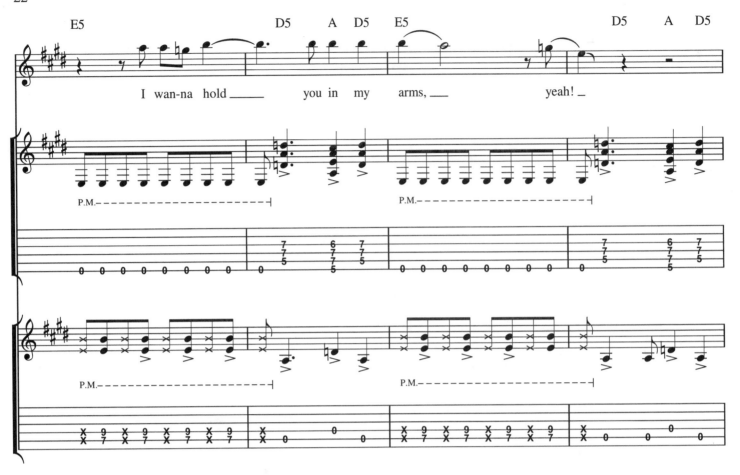

Chorus:

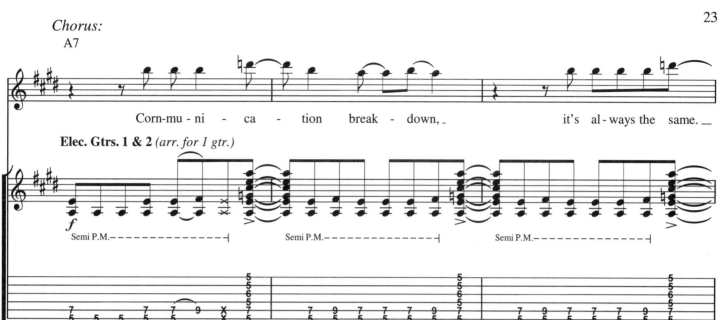

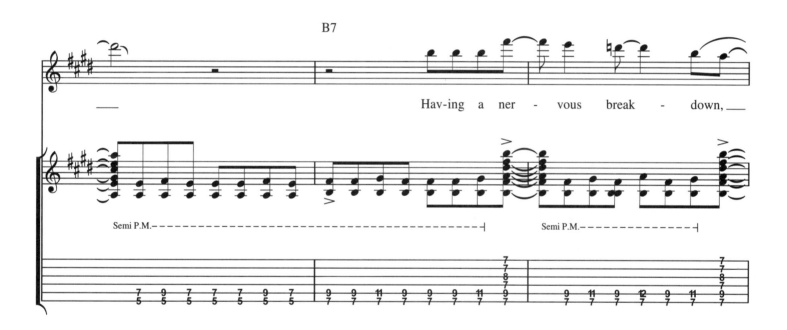

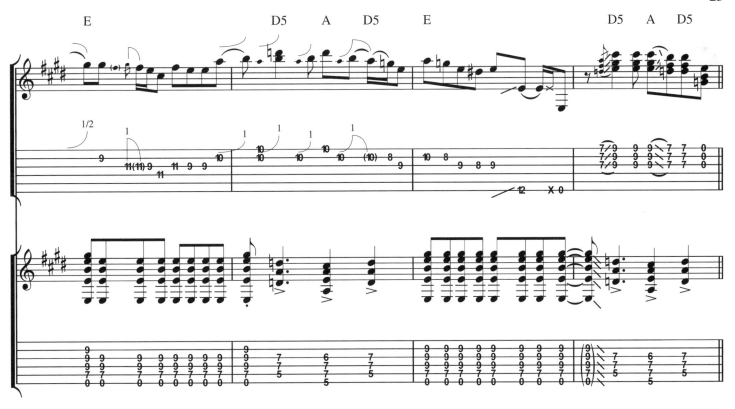

Chorus:

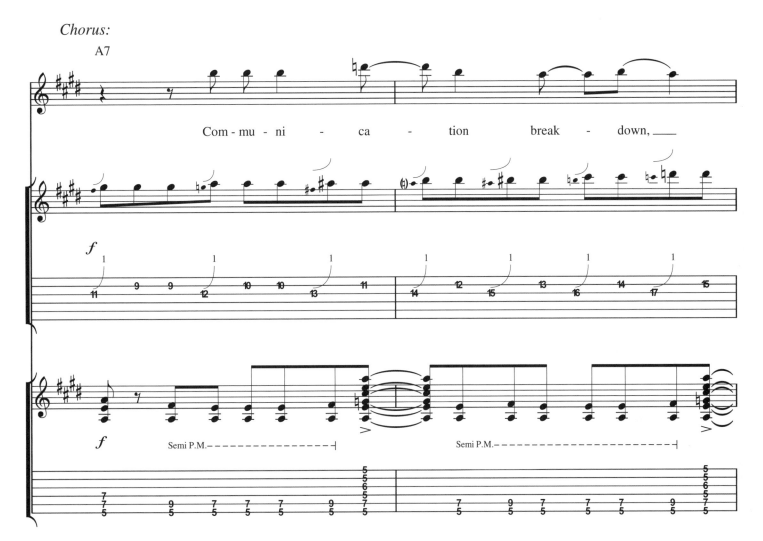

Com - mu - ni - ca - tion break - down, ___

DAZED AND CONFUSED

Words and Music by
JIMMY PAGE

Moderately slow ♩. = 158

Intro:

N.C.(Em)

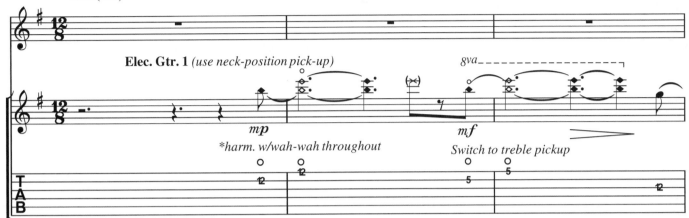

Elec. Gtr. 1 (use neck-position pick-up)

mp

mf

*harm. w/wah-wah throughout

Switch to treble pickup

Verse 1:
N.C.

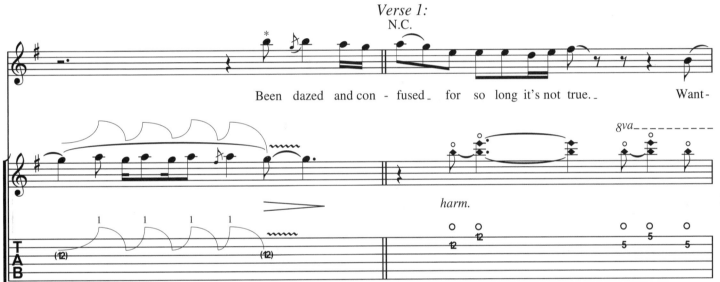

Been dazed and con - fused — for so long it's not true. — Want-

harm.

* See footnote at trio interlude before Verse 3 for an explanation
of the shifting meters of this song.

- ed a wom - an, nev-er bar-gained for you. ___   Lots of peo-ple talk - in', few of them know —

harm.

harm.

* Rock wah-wah pedal simile to the following rhythm figure. (+ = treble position, o = bass position)

Dazed and Confused - 14 - 1

soul of a wom-an was cre-at-ed be-low,___ yeah.___

Elec. Gtr. 1

Elec. Gtrs. 2 & 3
Rhy. Fig. 1

Upstemmed part played thuough fuzztone with octave effect (8va higher).
This can also be recreated with a pitch transposer.

You hurt___

end Rhy. Fig. 1

Even release

Dazed and Confused - 14 - 2

Verse 2:

____ and a-bused _ tell-in' all of your lies. _   Run 'round, _ sweet ba-by, Lord, __ how they hyp-no - tize. _

Elec. Gtr. 1 *(dbld.)*

Sweet lit-tle ba - by,   I don't know where you been. _   Gon-na love you, ba - by,   here I come a -

gain. _

Elec. Gtrs. 1 & 2

Elec. Gtr. 3
Rhy. Fig. 2   **end Rhy. Fig. 2**

w/Rhy. Fig. 1 *(Elec. Gtrs. 2 & 3)*

Ev-'ry

** Note: The original versions of this song by Jake Holmes and the Yardbirds clearly place the low E of the
signature bass line riff on beat 1 and the high G on beat 2. In the first two verses John Bonham chooses to
turn the meter around placing the high G on beat 2. From this point on he clearly turns the meter
around again, placing the high G on beat 2 as in the original versions. He remains in this meter for the
rest of the song. All live versions of this song follow this exact same pattern of turning the meter around.*

Verse 3:
w/Rhy. Fig. 1 *(Elec. Gtrs. 2 & 3)*

day I work so hard _ bring-in' home my hard-earned pay.   Try to love you ba-by, but you push me a-way. ____

Don't know where you're go-in', I don't know just where you've been;   sweet lit-tle ba-by I want _ you a-

* Overdubbed fill. Tremolo with bow and wah-wah.

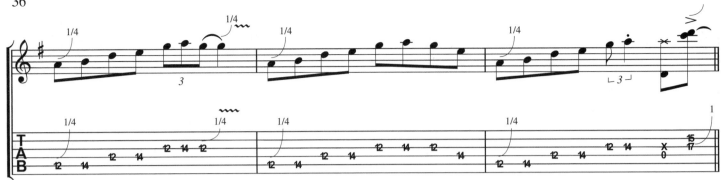

Guitar Solo

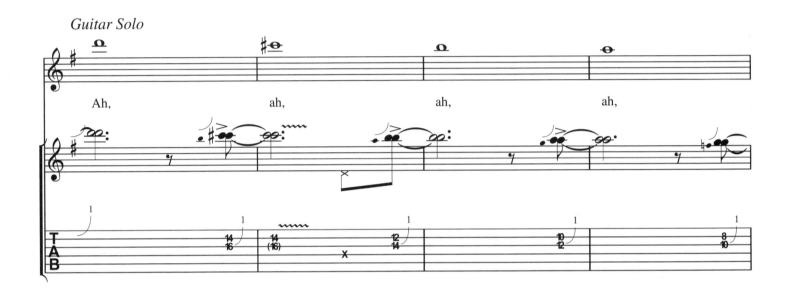

Ah,   ah,   ah,   ah,

ah,   ah,   ah,   ah,   ah,   ah,   ah. _____

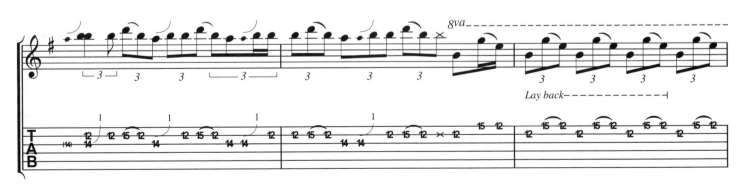

8va

Lay back ------------

Dazed and Confused - 14 - 9

Dazed and Confused - 14 - 11

* Upstemmed part with 8va fuzz.

Been dazed and con-fused for so long, it's not true, _

Lay back
mp

Guitar 3 tacet

want-ed a wom-an, nev-er bar-gained for you. _____ Take it eas-y, ba-by, let them say what they

will. ____ (Will your) tongue wag so much when I send you the

bill? _ Ooh, _____ yeah! ___ Al - right!

B5   N.C.   B5   N.C.   B5   N.C.   B5   N.C.

Elec. Gtr. 1

Elec. Gtr. 2

42

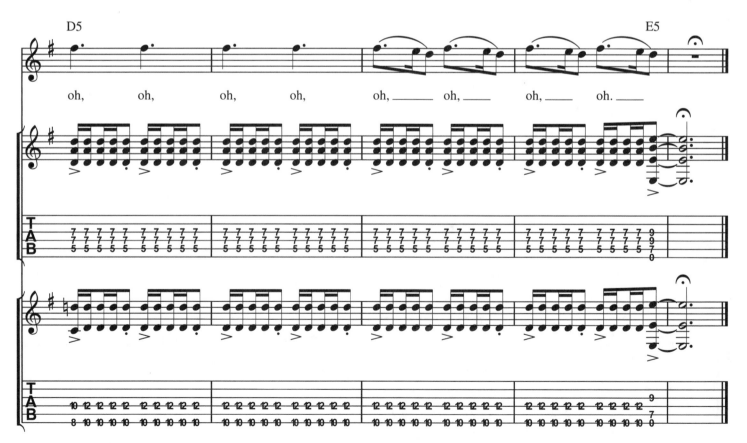

Dazed and Confused - 14 - 14

BABE I'M GONNA LEAVE YOU

Words and Music by
ANNE BREDON, JIMMY PAGE
and ROBERT PLANT

Moderately slow (half-time feel) ♩ = 138

Intro:

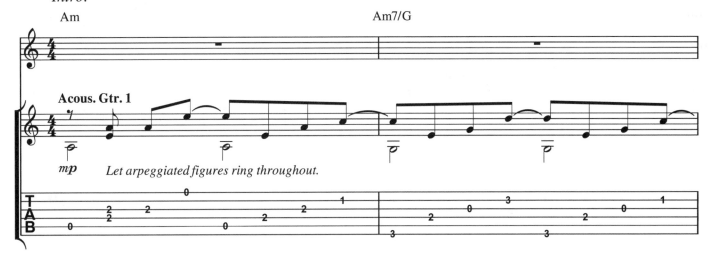

Let arpeggiated figures ring throughout.

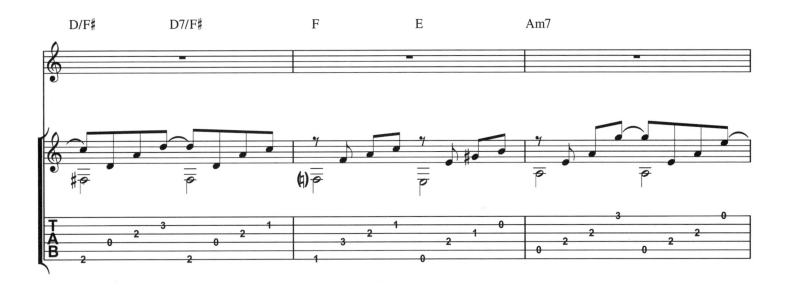

Babe I'm Gonna Leave You - 17 - 1

Verse 1:

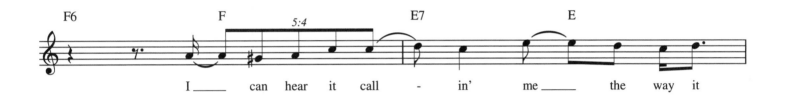

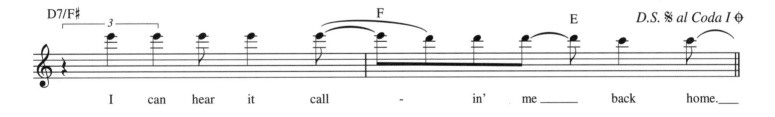

48

Coda I **w/Fill 2** *(Slide Gtr.)*

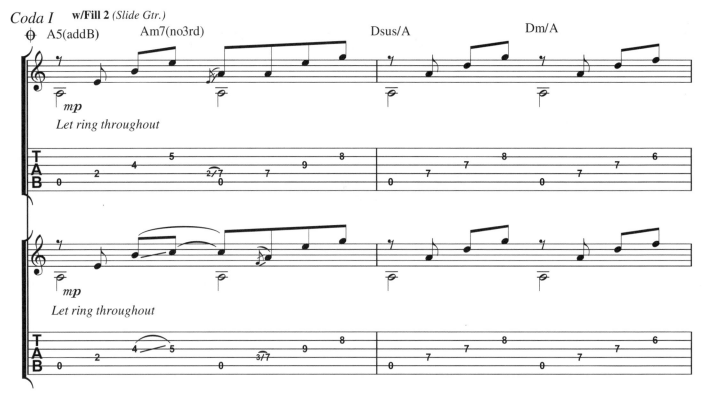

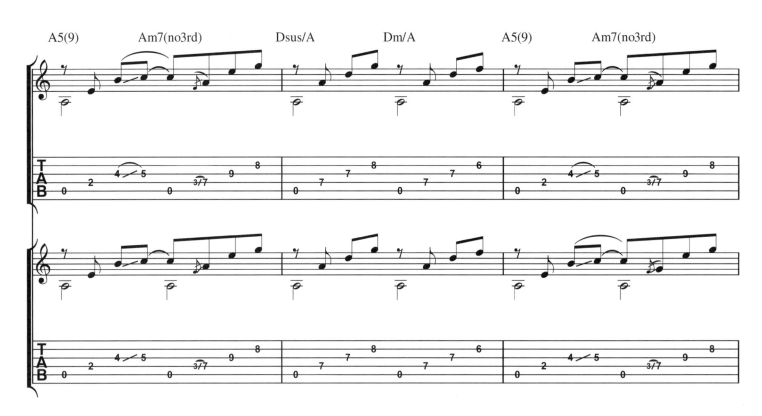

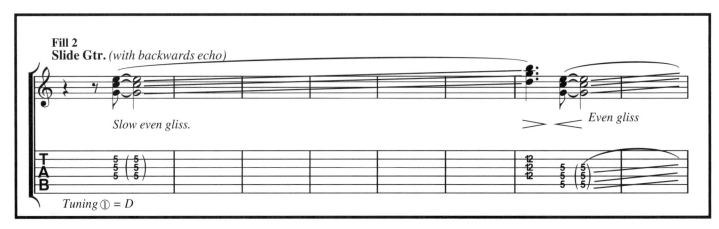

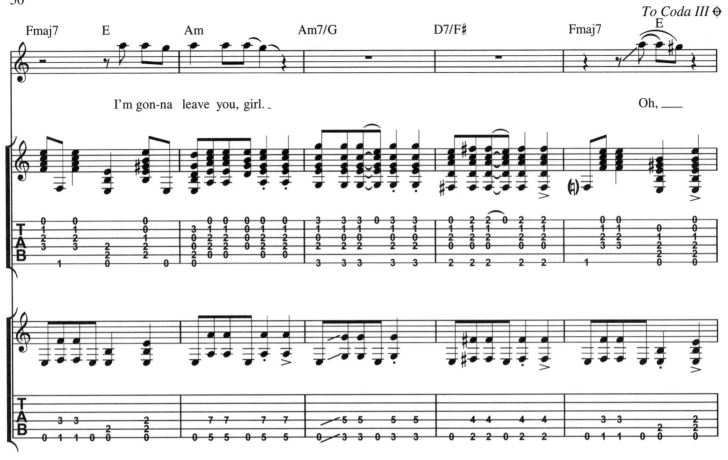

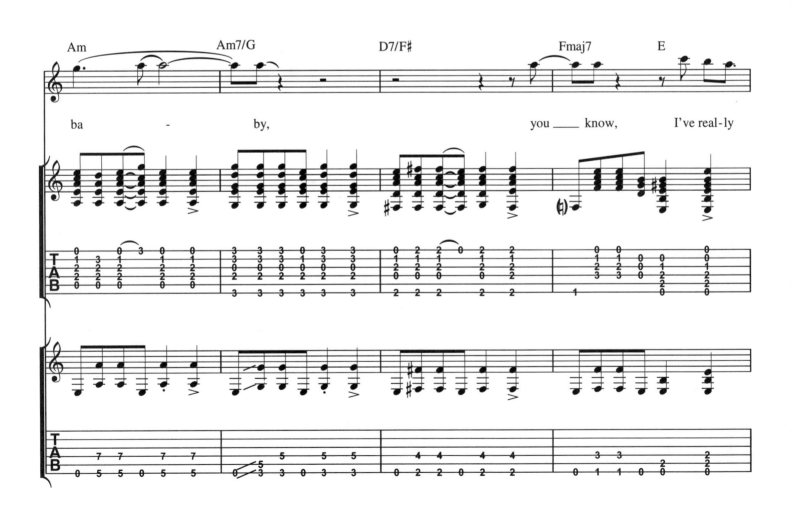

Coda II

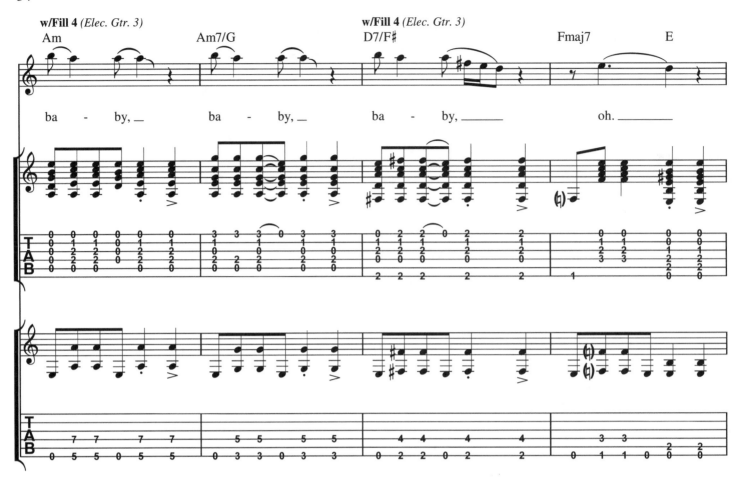

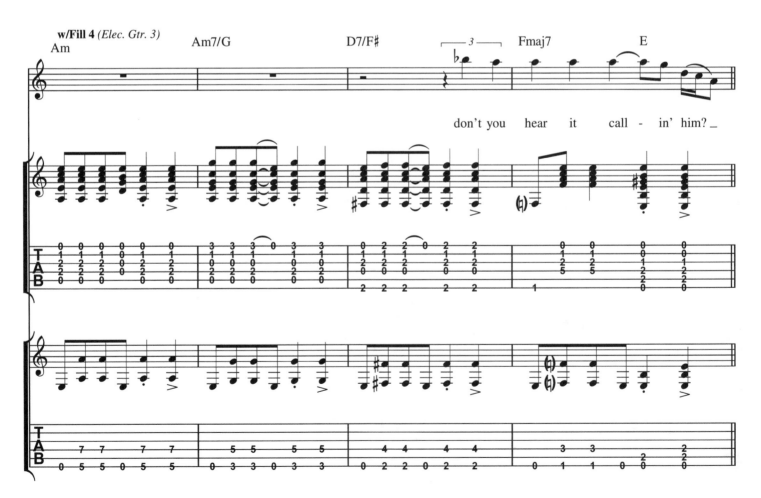

good to have you back a - gain and I know that one day, ba - by, __ it's real - ly gon-na

(Alternate fingering)

D.S.S. %% al Coda III

grow, _____ yes, it is. ___ We gon-na go walk-in' _ through the __ park _ ev - 'ry day.

Coda III

58

WHOLE LOTTA LOVE

Words and Music by
JIMMY PAGE, ROBERT PLANT,
JOHN PAUL JONES, JOHN BONHAM
and WILLIE DIXON

Moderately ♩ = 92

Intro:

Elec. Gtr. 1 *(w/dist.)*

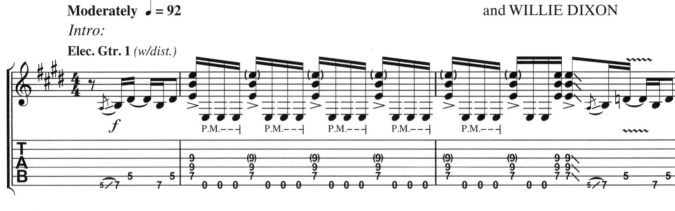

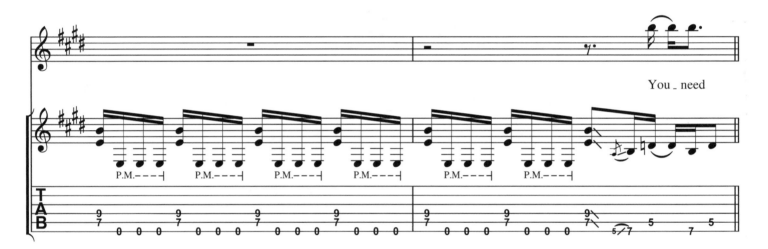

You _ need

Verse 1:

cool - in', _ um, ba-by, I'm not fool - in' _ I'm gon - na

Rhy. Fig. 1
simile

w/ Rhy. Fig. 1 *(Elec. Gtr. 1) 6 times*

send you _____ back to in'. ____

Whole Lotta Love - 9 - 1

Verse 2:
w/Rhy. Fig. 1 *(Elec. Gtr. 1) 8 times*

You been learn - in', and, ba - by, I mean

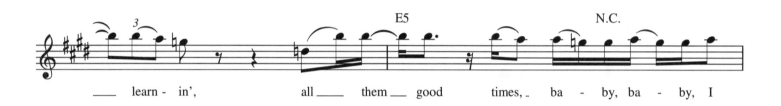

learn - in', all them good times, ba - by, ba - by, I

been a yearn - in', ah. Uh, way, way down in - side,

uh, hon - ey, you need ah. I'm gon - na give you my love, ah!

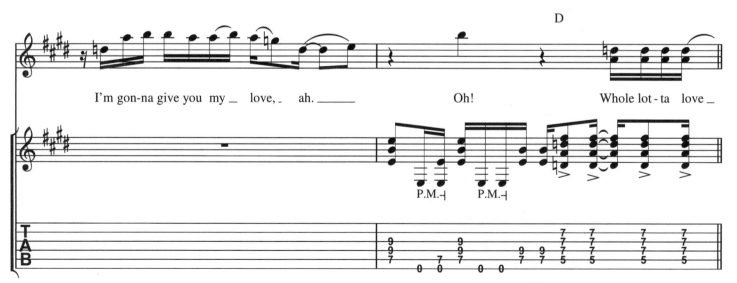

I'm gon - na give you my love, ah. Oh! Whole lot - ta love

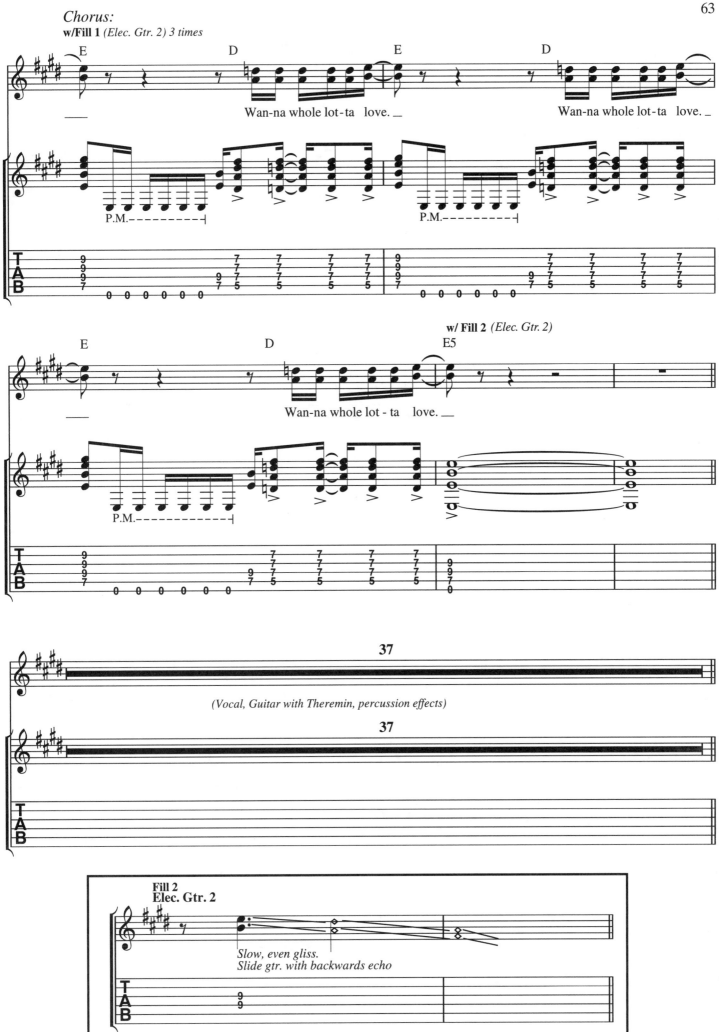

64

E5

Elec. Gtr. 1

Elec. Gtr. 3 *(w/dist.)*

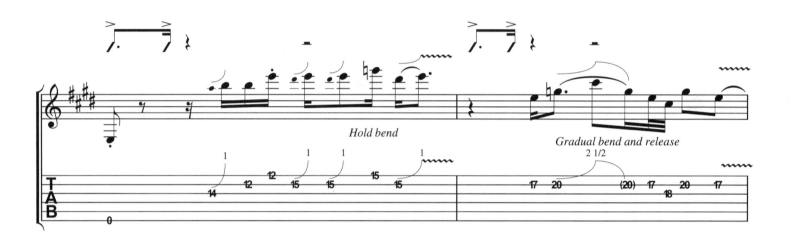

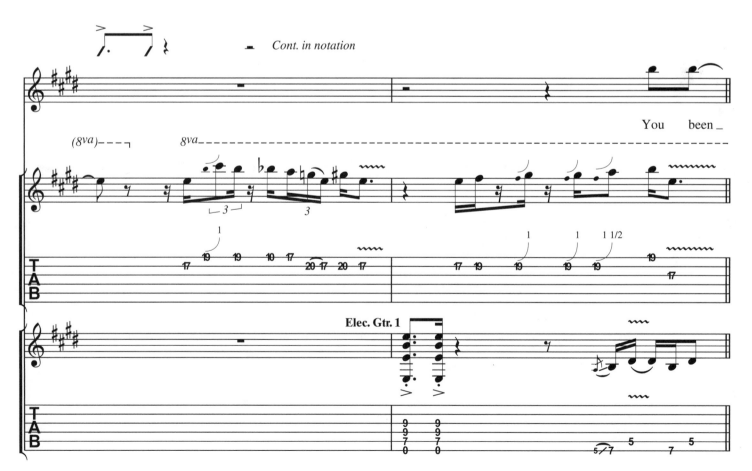

Cont. in notation

You been

Whole Lotta Love - 9 - 5

Verse 3:
w/Rhy. Fig. 1 *(Elec. Gtr. 1) 10 times*

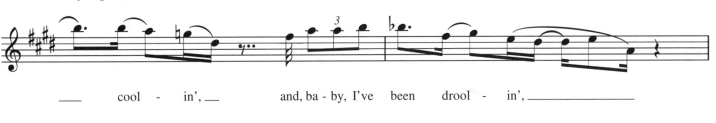

___ cool - in', ___ and, ba - by, I've been drool - in', _____

all ___ the good time, _ ba - by, I been ____ mis - us - in'. __

Uh, way, _ way _ down ___ in - side, ___ I'm gon-na give you my _ love.

I'm gon-na give you ev-'ry inch of my _ love. _ I'm gon-na give you my ___ love. _

Hey! ___ Al - right, _____ let's go! ___

Chorus:
w/Fill 1 *(Elec. Gtr. 2) 3 times*

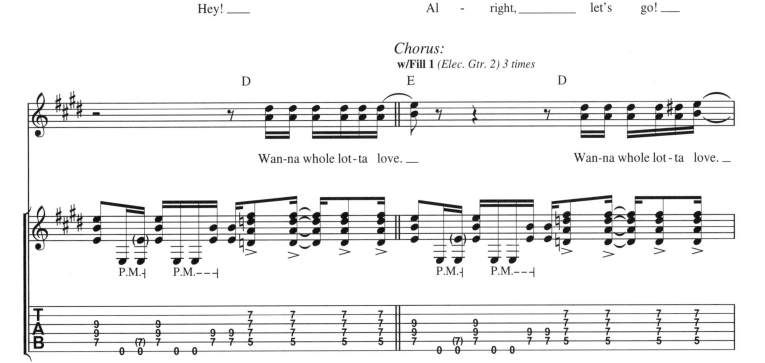

Wan-na whole lot-ta love. __ Wan-na whole lot-ta love. __

Whole Lotta Love - 9 - 6

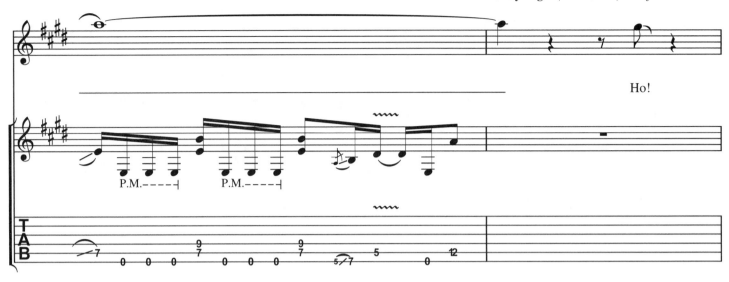

Ho!

Oh!   Oh!   Oh!   Whoa, ma, ma head!
(With echo repeats)

Keep it cool - in', ba - by!

Uh, keep it cool - in', ba - by!   Uh, keep it cool - in', ba - by!

Uh, keep it cool - in', ba - by!   Uh!   Ah!

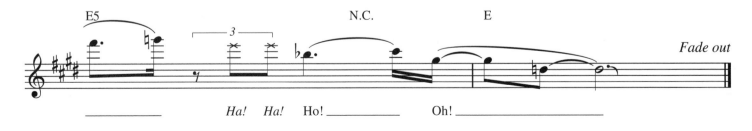

Fade out

Ha! Ha! Ho!   Oh!

RAMBLE ON

Words and Music by
JIMMY PAGE and ROBERT PLANT

Moderately ♩ = 98

Intro:

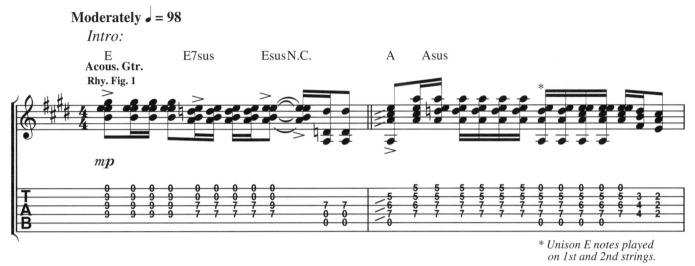

** Unison E notes played
on 1st and 2nd strings.*

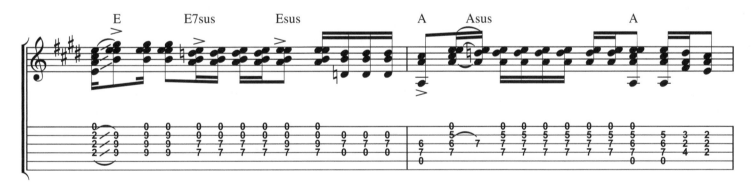

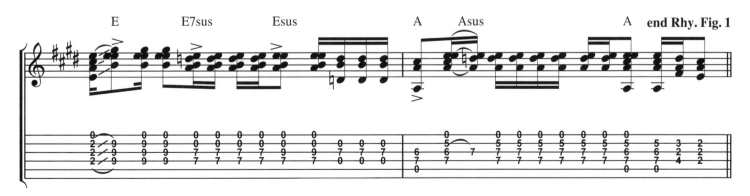

Ramble On - 10 - 1

Verse 1:

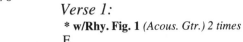

* w/Rhy. Fig. 1 *(Acous. Gtr.)* 2 times

Leaves are fall-in' all a-round, (it's) time I was on my way. _____

* *Features ad lib. variations of basic figure.*
Chord symbols outline basic harmony.

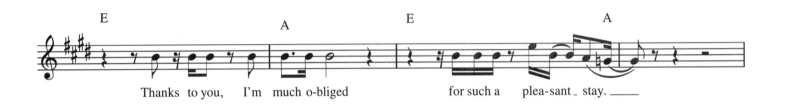

Thanks to you, I'm much o-bliged for such a plea-sant _ stay. _____

But now it's time for me to go, _____ the au-tumn moon _ lights _ my way. _

But now I smell the rain _ (and) with it pain, and it's head-ed my way. _

Pre-chorus:

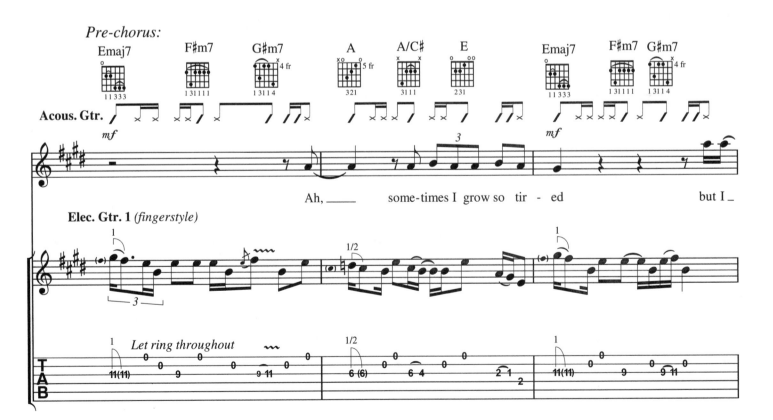

Ah, _____ some-times I grow so tir-ed but I _

Elec. Gtr. 1 *(fingerstyle)*

Ramble On - 10 - 2

Chorus:

Ram - ble   on. _____   Find the   queen _____   of   all ___   my   dreams _

Verse 2:

w/Rhy. Fig. 1 *(Acous. Gtr.)*

Got no time to spend and   weep,   the time   has come   to be   gone. __

Elec. Gtr. 1

(and) though   our health _ we drank   a thou-sand times,   it's time to ram-ble on. __

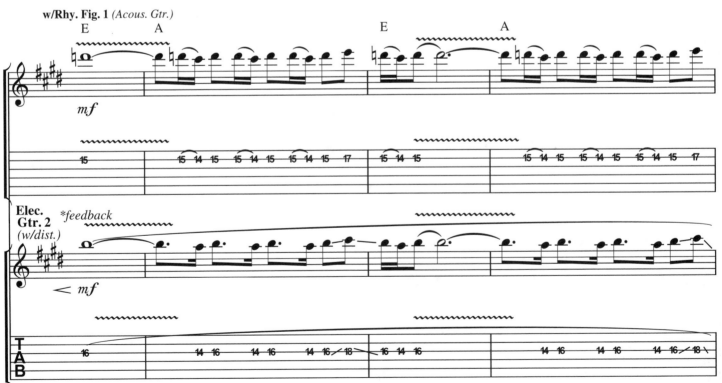

w/Rhy. Fig. 1 *(Acous. Gtr.)*

mf

Elec. Gtr. 2 *feedback*
(w/dist.)

< mf

*Fade in feedback on fundamental

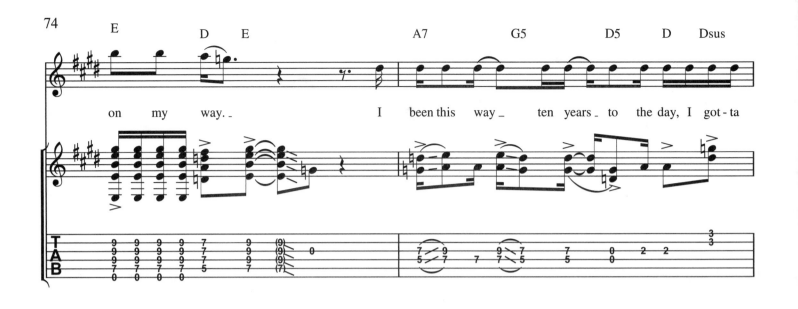

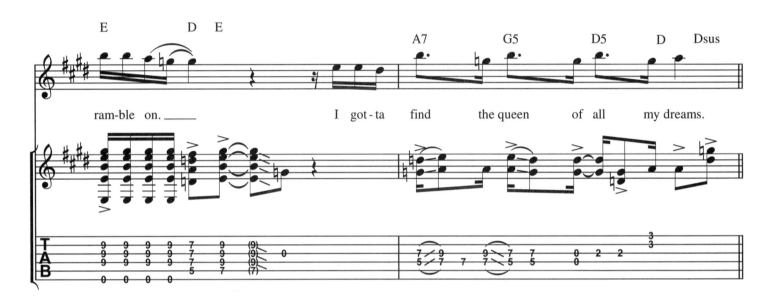

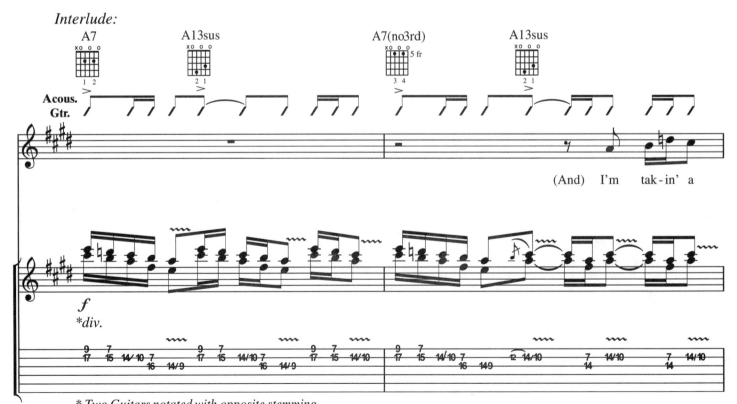

* *Two Guitars notated with opposite stemming.*
  Downstems notated to right of / in TAB when necessary.

Verse 3:

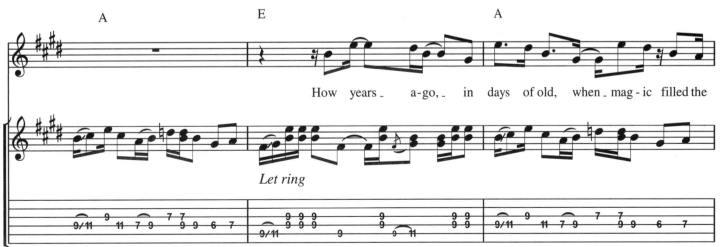

w/Rhy. Fig. 1 *(Acous. Gtr.)*

air. ___   'Twas in the dark - est depths of

Mor - dor,   I met a girl so fair, _____   but Gol-lum and the e - vil one _

crept up and slipped a - way with her, _ her, __ her, _ her, _ her, _ yeah. _____

Pre-chorus:

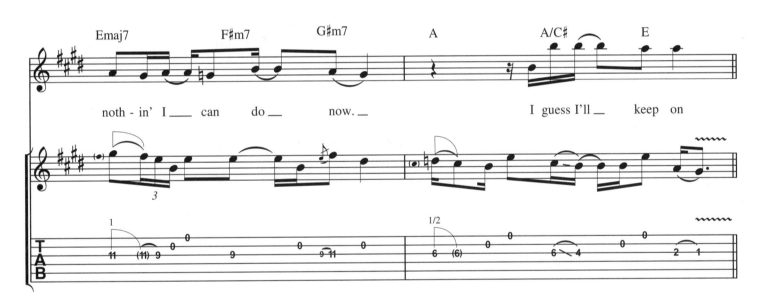

Chorus:

w/Rhy. Figs. 2 & 3*(Acous. Gtr. & Elec. Gtr. 1) 12 times*

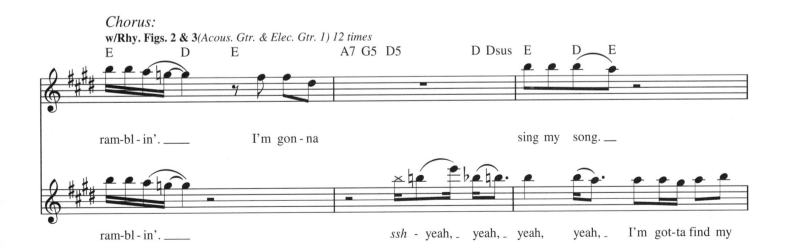

HEARTBREAKER

**Words and Music by
JIMMY PAGE, ROBERT PLANT,
JOHN PAUL JONES, and JOHN BONHAM**

Moderately ♩ = 98

Intro:

Play 3 times

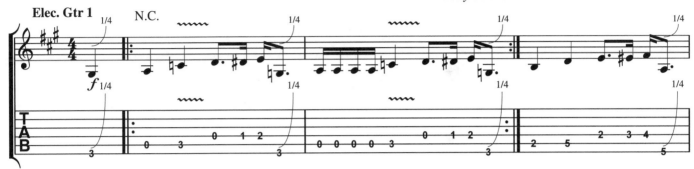

Verse 1:

Hey, fel-las, have you heard the news, _ you know that An-nie's back _ in town. _ It

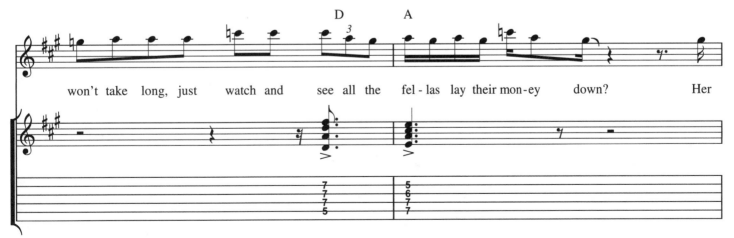

won't take long, just watch and see all the fel-las lay their mon-ey down? Her

Heartbreaker - 10 - 1

Verse 2:

Well,
it's been ten years and — may-be more since I first set eyes — on you. The
best years of my life — gone by, — here I am a-lone and blue. Some peo-ple cry and — some peo-ple die by
the wick-ed ways of love. — But I'll just keep — on roll-in' a-long — with the

IMMIGRANT SONG

Words and Music by
JIMMY PAGE and ROBERT PLANT

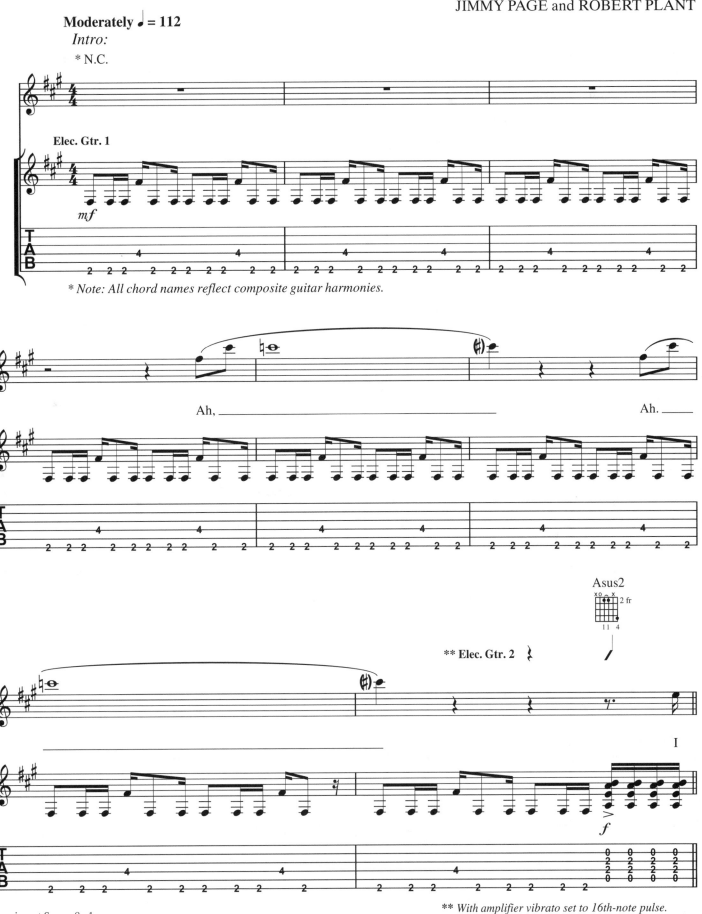

Immigrant Song - 8 - 1

Cont. in notation

com - ing

On we sweep with, with thresh-ing oar,

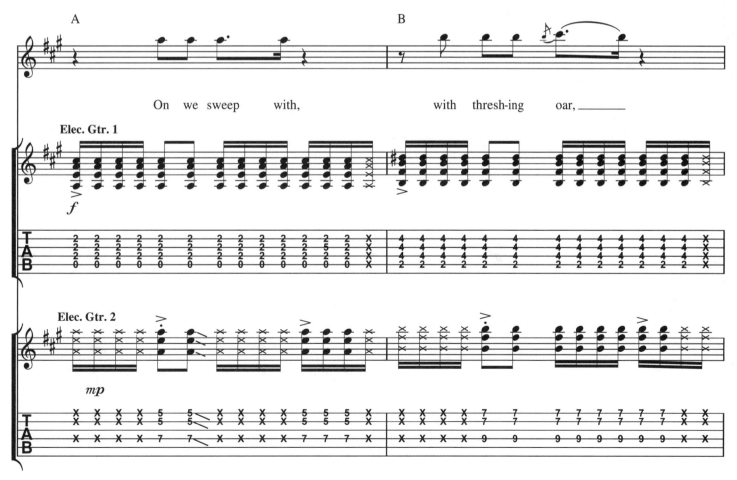

C

our on - ly goal   will be the   west - ern __ shore. __

div. *

* Overdub

Interlude:

F#(2)

Elec. Gtr. 2 cont. simile

Ah, _____

Elec. Gtr. 1

mf

__   Ah. _____   We

A5

f

Verse 2:
Elec. Gtr. 2 cont. verse rhy. simile

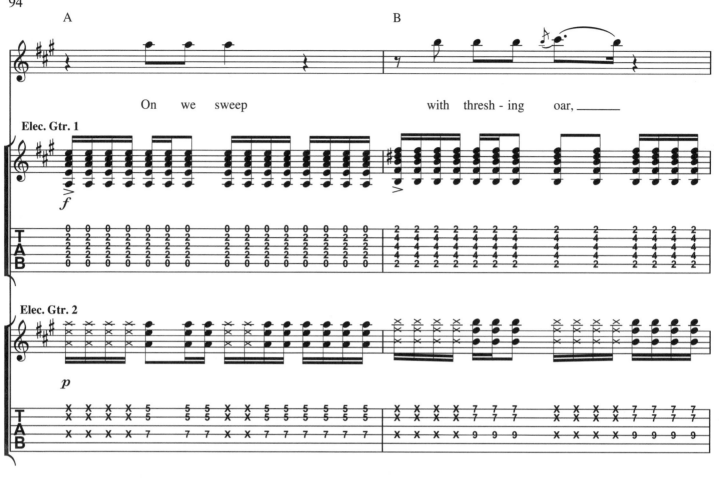

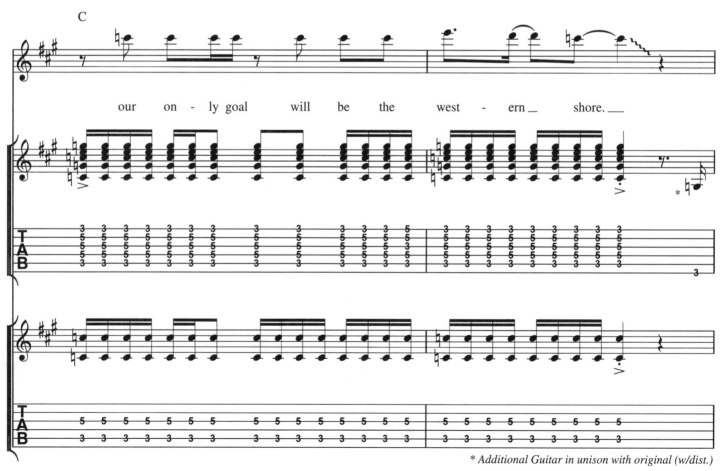

Additional Guitar in unison with original (w/dist.)

SINCE I'VE BEEN LOVING YOU

Words and Music by
JIMMY PAGE, ROBERT PLANT
and JOHN PAUL JONES

Since I've Been Loving You - 14 - 1

100

Verse 2:

*Fuzztone out.

Since I've Been Loving You - 14 - 4

tell,   let me tell you I real-ly did the   best I   could.

Fm7

I've been, I've been work-ing from sev - en,

ah, to e - lev - en ev - 'ry night, _ I said it kind - a makes my

Cm7

life a drag,   drag, drag,   drag,   Lord, _____

* Add fuzztone.
** Fuzztone out.

Guitar Solo:

* Add fuzztone.

*Fuzztone out.

Since I've Been Loving You - 14 - 9

Verse 3:

Do you re-mem-ber, ma-ma, when I knocked up-on your door, I said you had the nerve

to help? You did-n't want me no more, __ yeah. __

O-pen my front door, hear my back door slam, you know I must have

one of them new fan-gled, new _ fan-gled back door men, yeah, yeah, yeah, yeah, yeah, yeah.

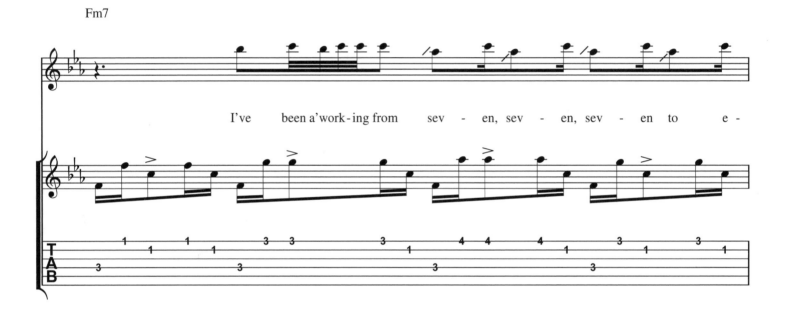

I've been a'work-ing from sev - en, sev - en, sev - en to e-

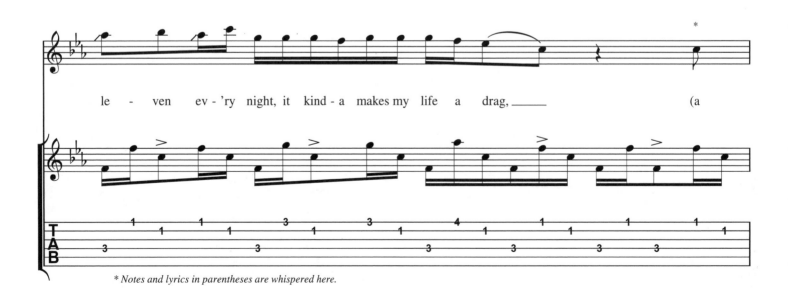

le - ven ev - 'ry night, it kind - a makes my life a drag, _____ (a

Notes and lyrics in parentheses are whispered here.

*Fuzztion out.
**Slide down and up repeatedly.

ROCK AND ROLL

Words and Music by
JIMMY PAGE, ROBERT PLANT,
JOHN PAUL JONES and JOHN BONHAM

Heavy rock and roll, briskly ♩ = 170

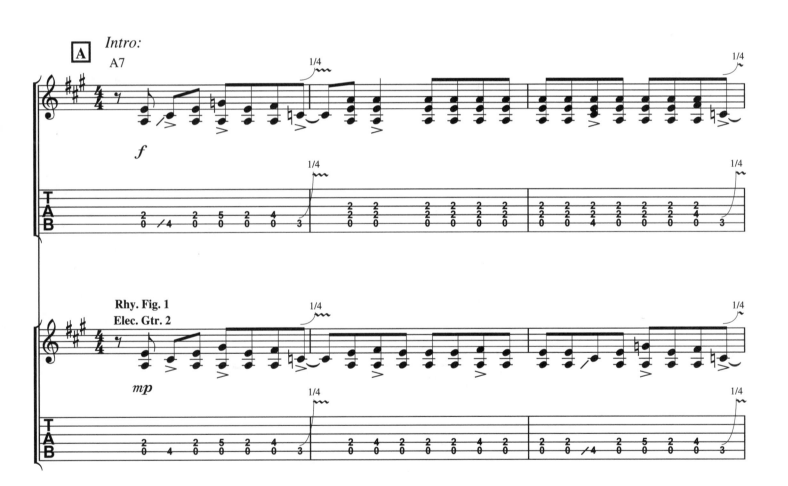

Rock and Roll - 11 - 1

been a long time, been a long time, been a long lone - ly, lone - ly, lone - ly, lone - ly, lone - ly

end Rhy. Fig. 2

Let the 6th string ring.

time. Yes, it has. ____ 2. It's

Elec. Gtr. 1

Elec. Gtr. 2

Elec. Gtr. 3

Rock and Roll - 11 - 5

E *Guitar Solo:*
w/ Rhy. Fig. 2 *(Elec. Gtrs. 1 & 2)*

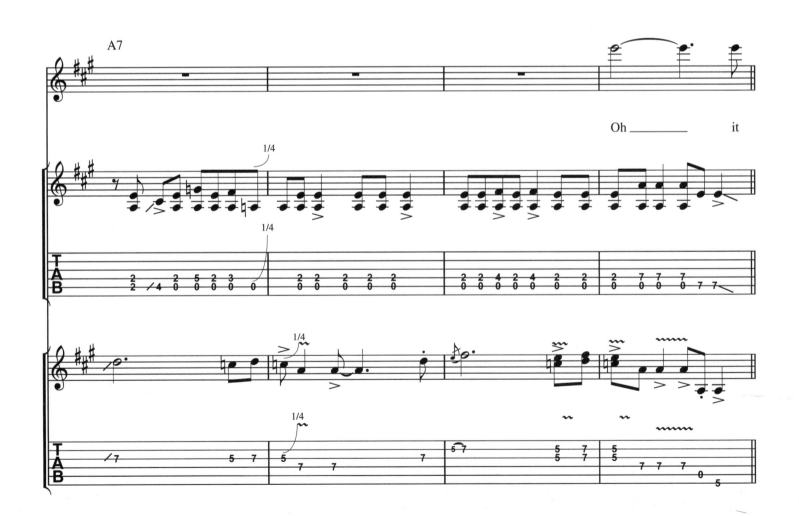

Oh _____ it

G Outro:

BLACK DOG

Words and Music by
JIMMY PAGE, ROBERT PLANT
and JOHN PAUL JONES

Hard blues rock
Intro:

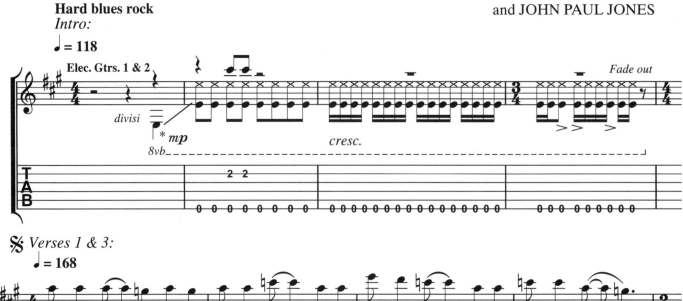

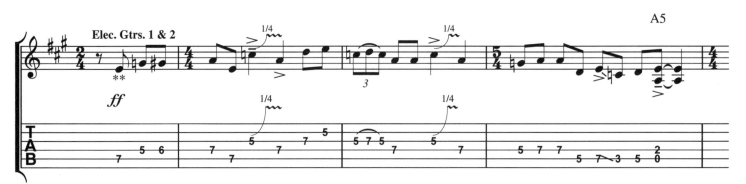

1. Hey, hey, ma - ma, said the way you move, gon-na make you sweat, gon-na make you groove,
f 3. *See additional lyrics*

A5

*This pitch is from a tape effect and not playable.
**Enter on drummer's cue.

Uh-huh, child, way you shake that thing, gon-na make you burn, gon-na make you sting.

Black Dog - 14 - 1

Heh, hey, ba - by, when you walk that way, __ watch your hon-ey drip, __ can't keep a - way. __

Chorus:

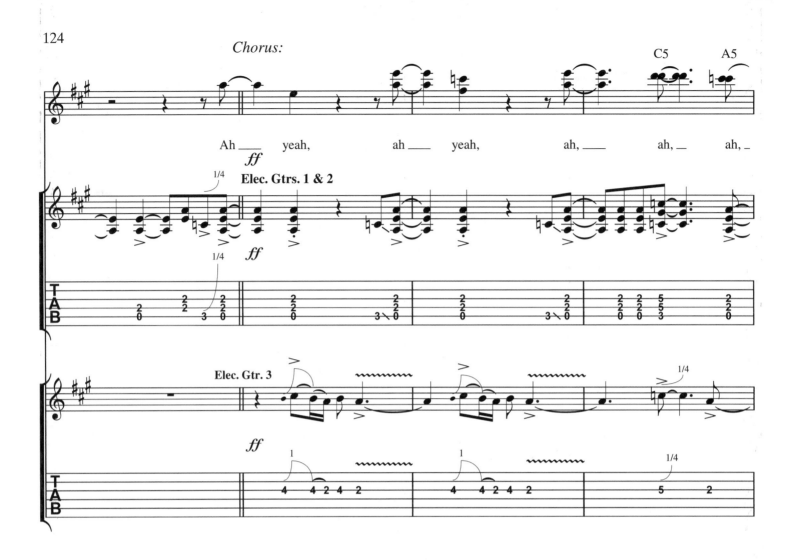

Verses 2 & 4:

2. I got-ta roll, can't stand still, _ got a flame-in' heart, _ can't get my _ fill.
4. *See additional lyircs*

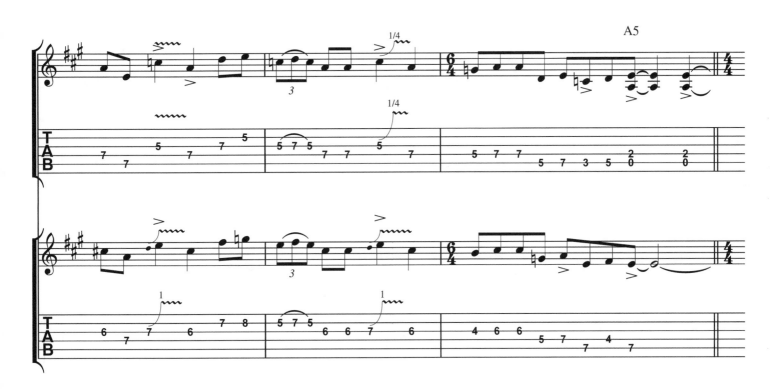

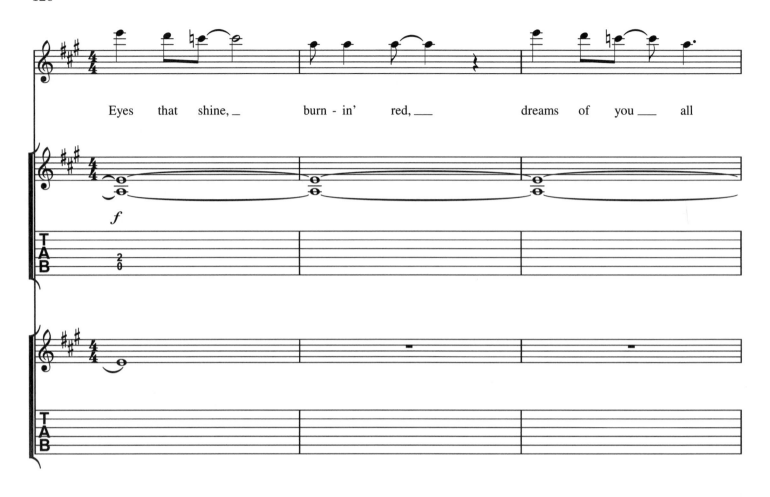

Eyes that shine, __ burn - in' red, __ dreams of you __ all

through my head. ___

Bridge:

A5

Ah   ah   ah   ah

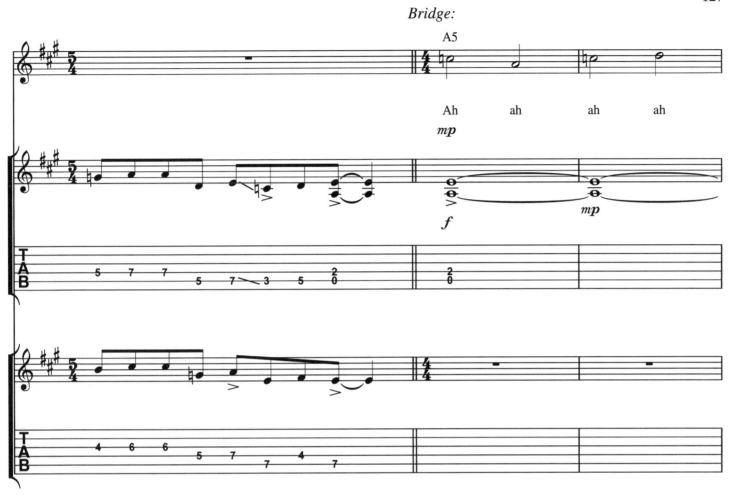

To Coda ⊕

ah   ah   ah   ah   ah   ah   ah   ah

* Feedback harmonic

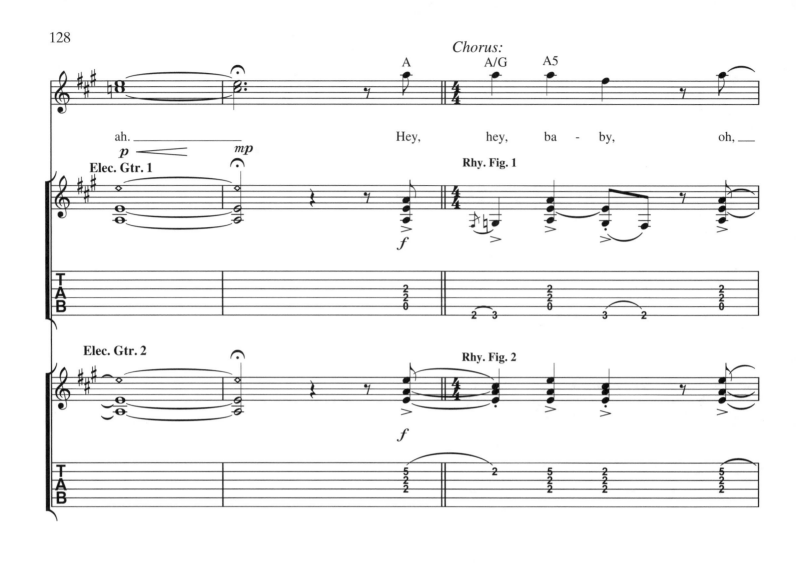

The note E is played here by the Bass guitar only.

2. Did-n't

Crescendo on upper note in vocal, decrescendo on the lower note.
**Elec. Gtr. 3 is recorded through a Leslie speaker, and on a separate track with a standard amplifier.*

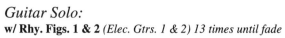

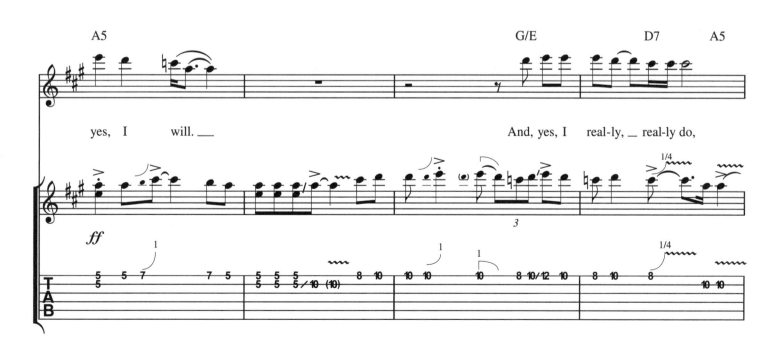

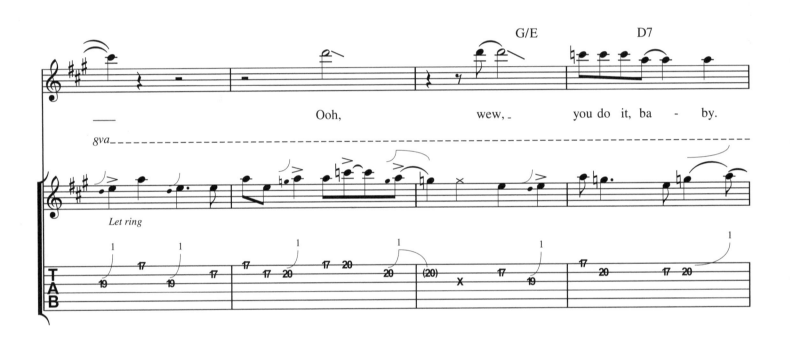

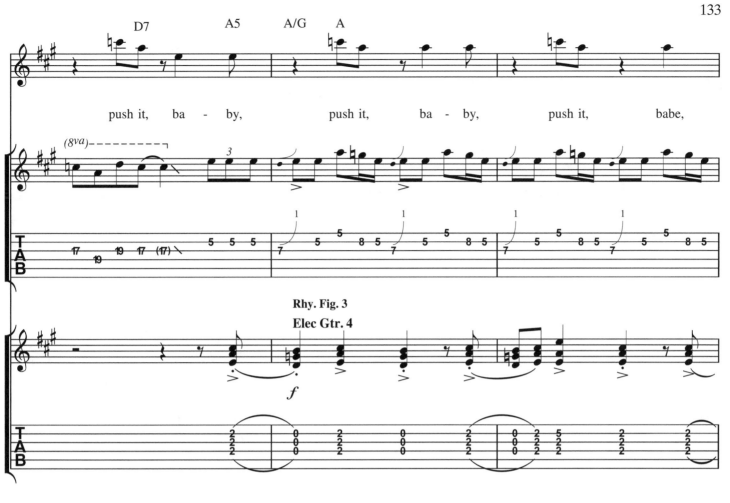

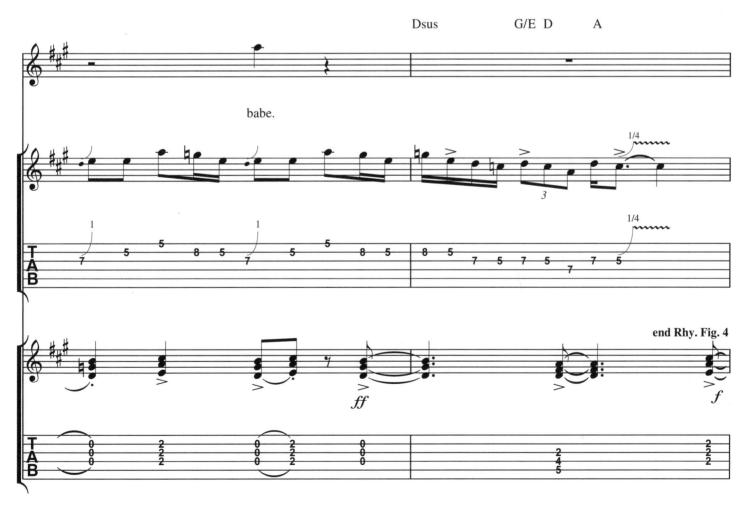

I'd real-ly like to do it now.

Fade

I'd real-ly like to do it now.

Verse 3
Didn't take too long 'fore I found out what
People mean by down and out.

Spent my money, took may car,
Start tellin' her friends she gonna be a star.

I don't know, but I been told,
I big-legged woman ain't got no soul.
(To Chorus:)

Verse 4:
All I ask, all I pray,
Steady loaded woman gonna come my way.

Need a woman gonna hold my hand,
Will tell me no lies, make me a happy man.
Ah ah ah ah ah ah ah ah ah ah ah ah ah.
(To Coda)

WHEN THE LEVEE BREAKS

Words and Music by
JIMMY PAGE, ROBERT PLANT,
JOHN PAUL JONES, JOHN BONHAM
and MEMPHIS MINNIE

* All gtrs. in Open G tuning down 1 whole step:

6= C 3= F
5= F 2= A
4= C 1= C

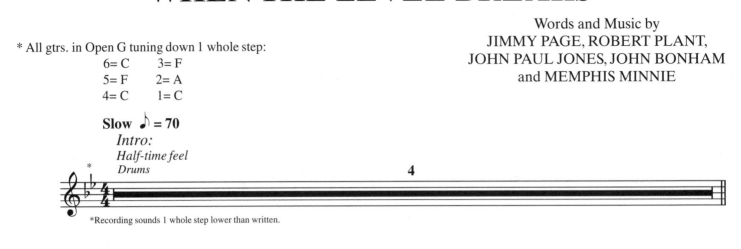

Slow ♪ = 70

Intro:
Half-time feel
Drums

4

*Recording sounds 1 whole step lower than written.

𝄋 *Harmonica Solo:*

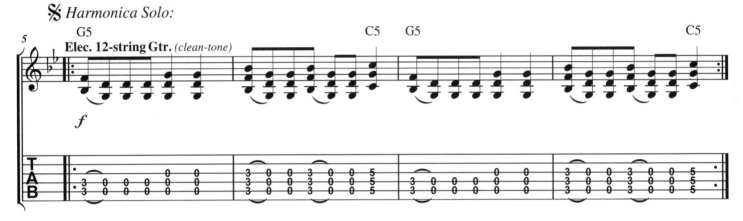

Elec. 12-string Gtr. *(clean-tone)*

Play 3 times

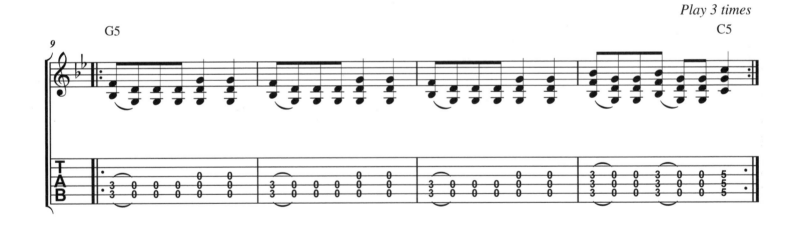

Rhy. Fig. 1

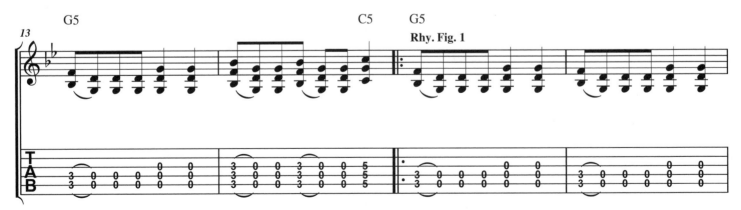

When the Levee Breaks - 9 - 1

138

le - vee breaks, ___ have no place ___ to stay. _____
le - vee breaks, ___ ma - ma, you got ___ to move. _____ Ah, ooo, ___ ooo.

Verses 2 & 4: (1:48), (4:33)
w/Rhy. Fig. 1 *(Elec. 12-string Gtr.) 3 times, simile*

2. Mean old ___ le - vee ___ taught me to weep ___ and moan. ____
4. All last night, sat on the le - vee and

mean old le - vee taught me to weep ___ and moan. _____ It's
moaned. _____ All ___ last night sat on the le - vee ___ and moaned. ___

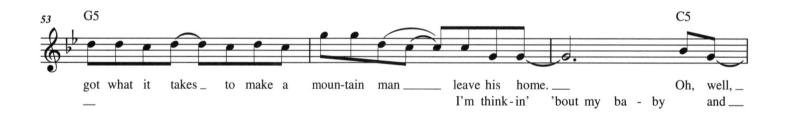

got what it takes ___ to make a moun - tain man _____ leave his home. ___ Oh, well, ___
___ I'm think - in' 'bout my ba - by and ___

w/Rhy. Fig. 2 *(Elec. 12-string Gtr.) simile*

___ oh, well, ___ oh, well, _____ ooo. ___
___ my hap - py home. ___ Oh, ___ oh.

Interlude: (2:12)
w/Rhy. Fig. 3 *(Elec. 12-string Gtr.) 2 times, simile*

To Coda ⊕

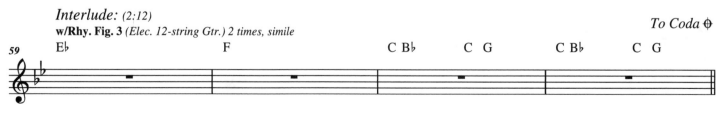

go - in' down south, they got no work to do if ya' goin' on ta Chi - ca - go. __

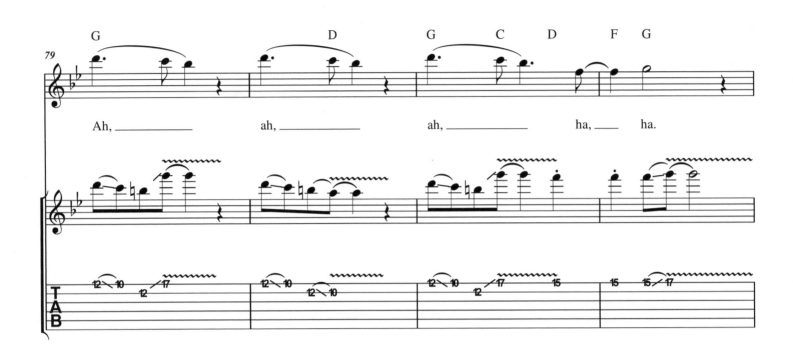

Ah, _____ ah, _____ ah, _____ ha, __ ha.

D.S. ℅ al Coda

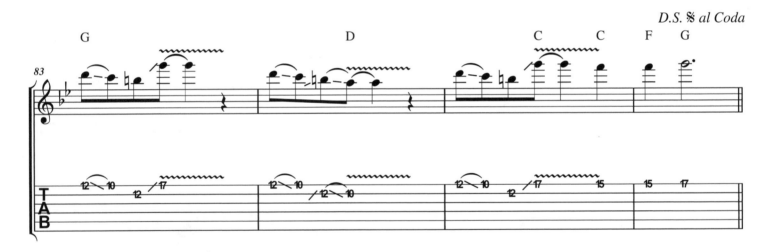

Coda

(5:09)

w/Riff A *(Elec. 6-string Gtr.) 2 times*

Elec. 12-string Gtr.

Rhy. Fig. 5

end Rhy. Fig. 5

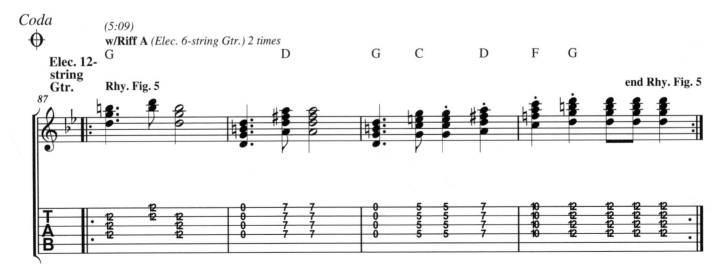

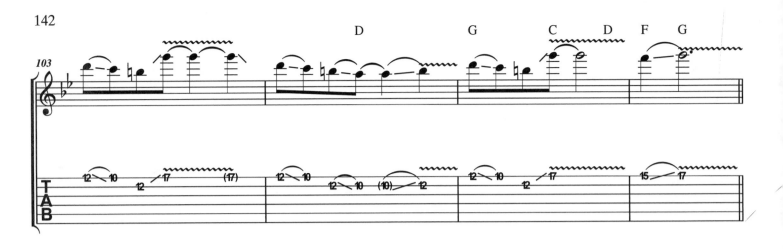

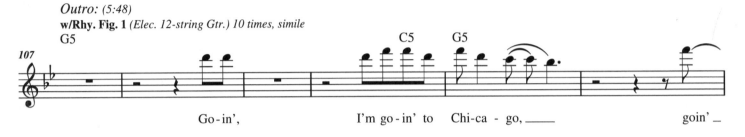

Outro: (5:48)
w/Rhy. Fig. 1 *(Elec. 12-string Gtr.) 10 times, simile*

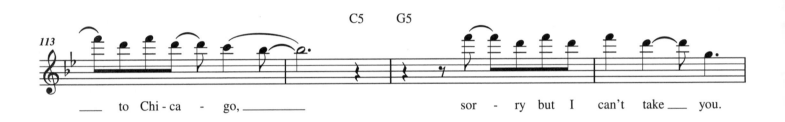

Go-in',   I'm go-in' to Chi-ca-go, _____   goin' _____

_____ to Chi-ca-go, _____   sor - ry but I can't take ___ you.

w/ misc. backwards echo and panning effects *(Elec. 6 & 12-string Gtrs.) till end*

Ah, ___   go-in' down,   I'm go-in' down now.   Go-in' down,   I'm go-in'

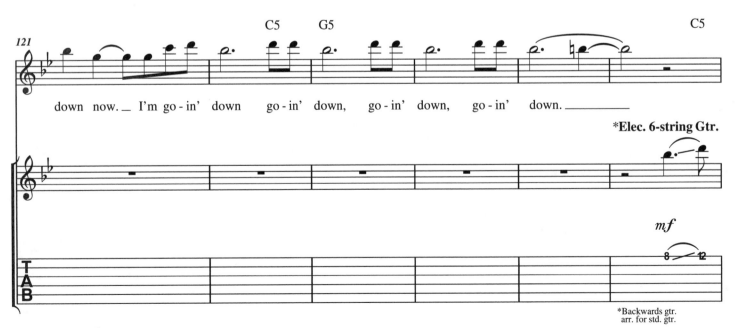

down now. ___ I'm go-in' down   go-in' down,   go-in' down,   go-in' down. _____

Elec. 6-string Gtr.

mf

*Backwards gtr.
arr. for std. gtr.

STAIRWAY TO HEAVEN

Words and Music by
JIMMY PAGE and ROBERT PLANT

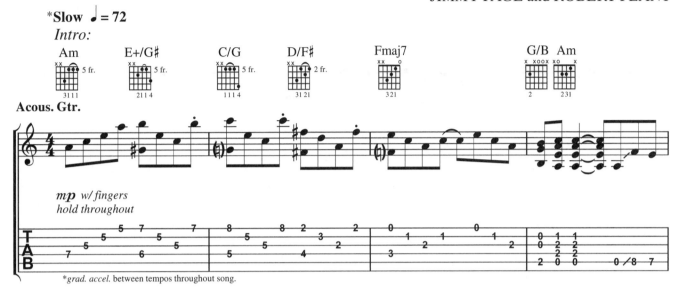

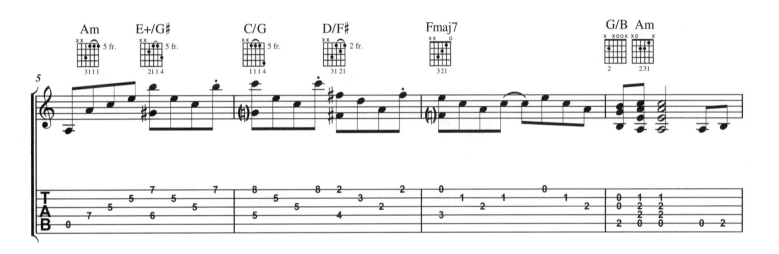

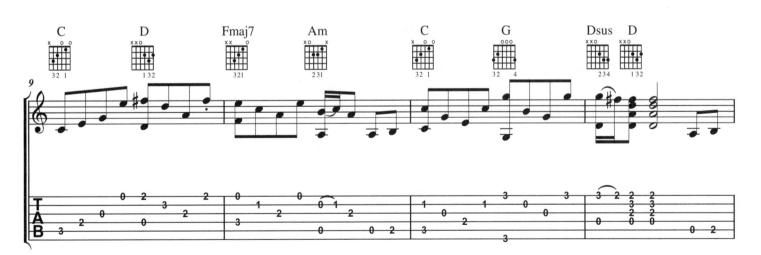

Stairway to Heaven - 16 - 1

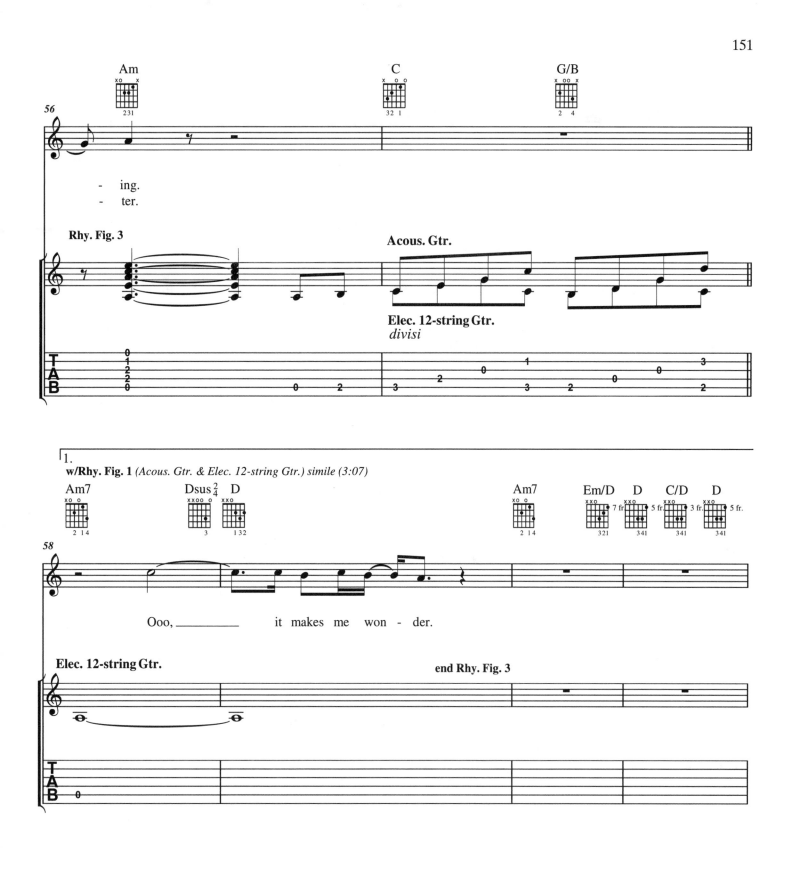

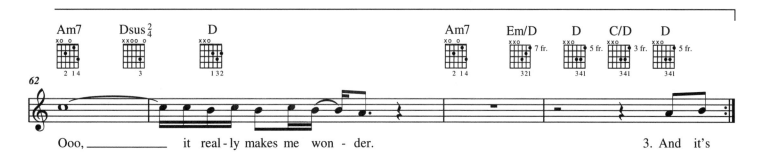

152

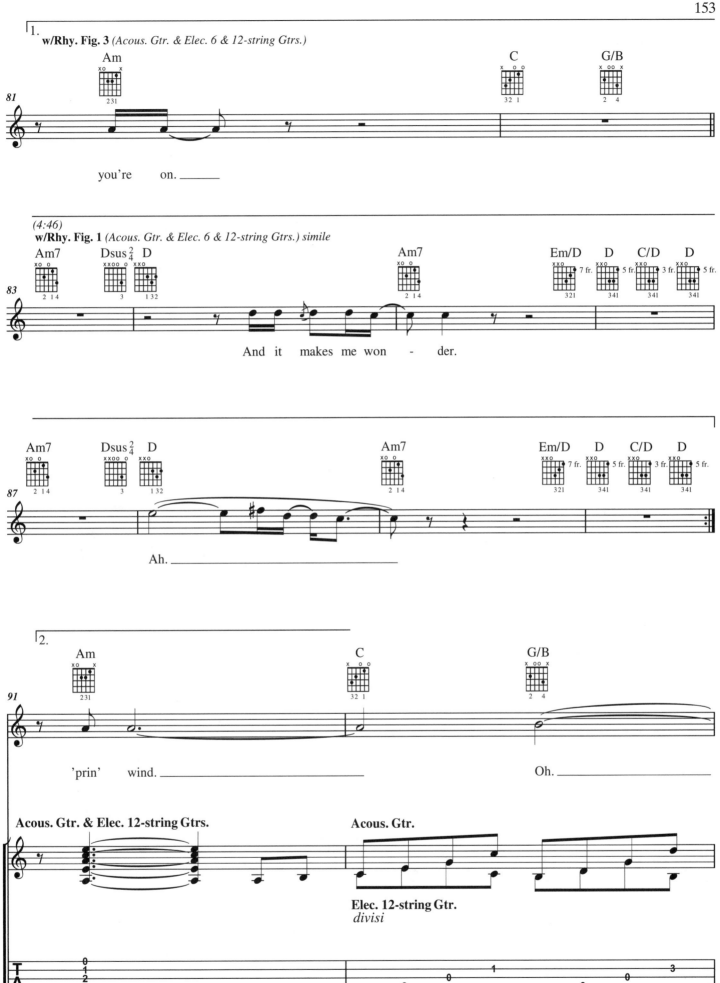

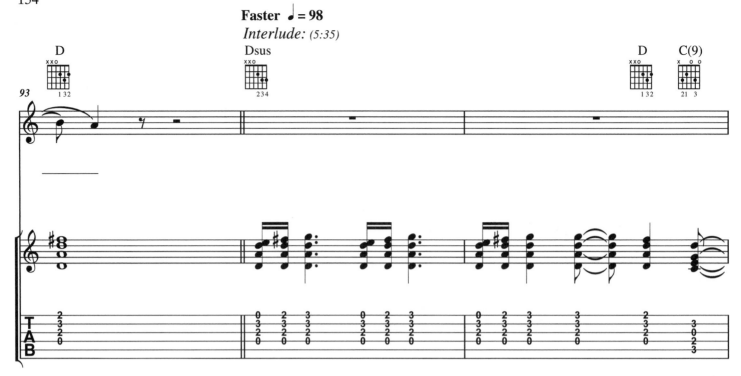

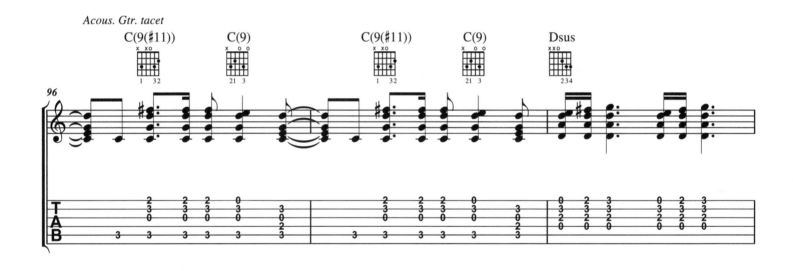

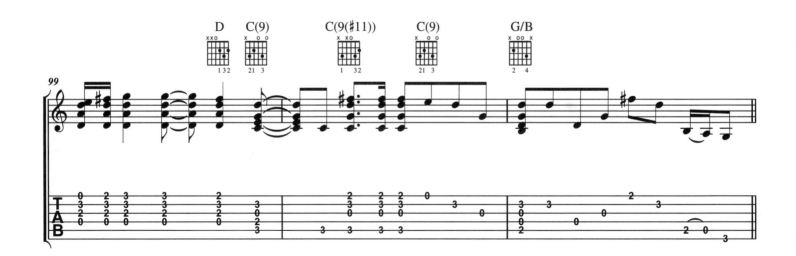

Guitar Solo: (5:56)

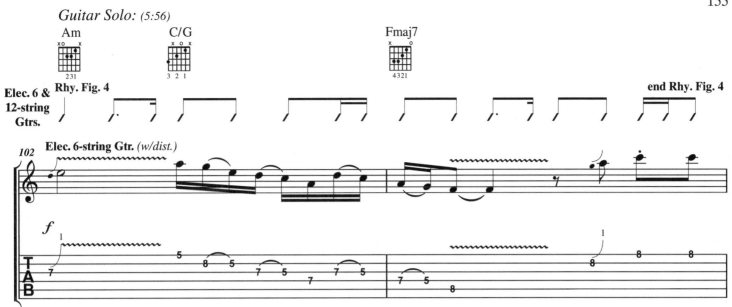

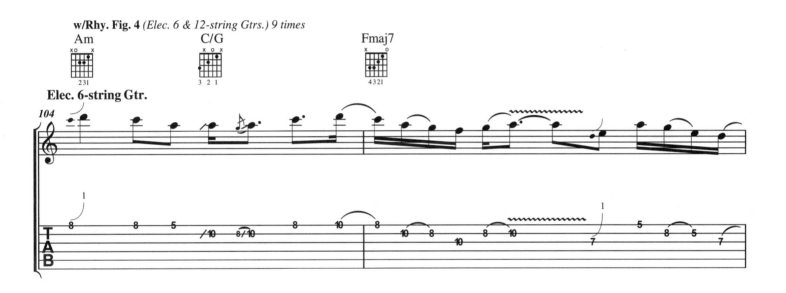

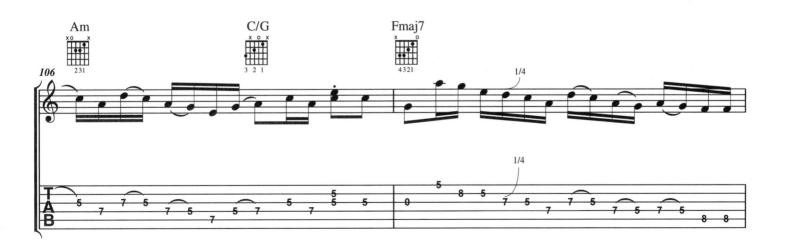

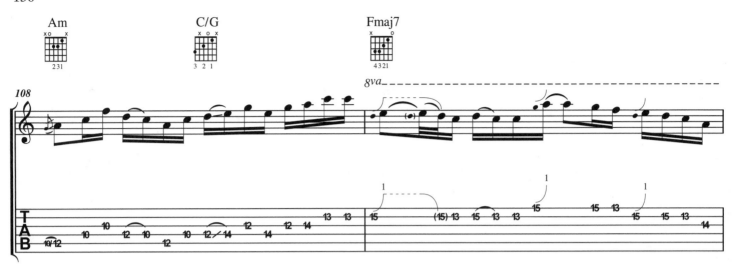

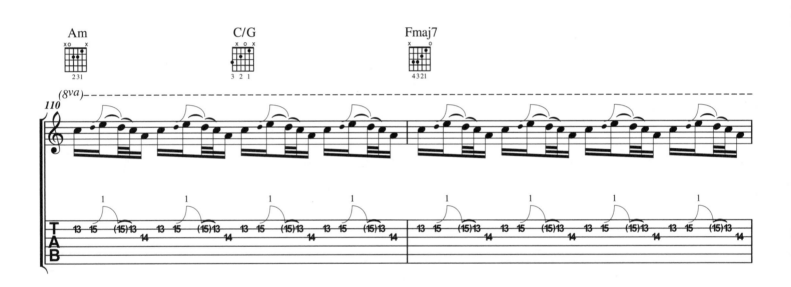

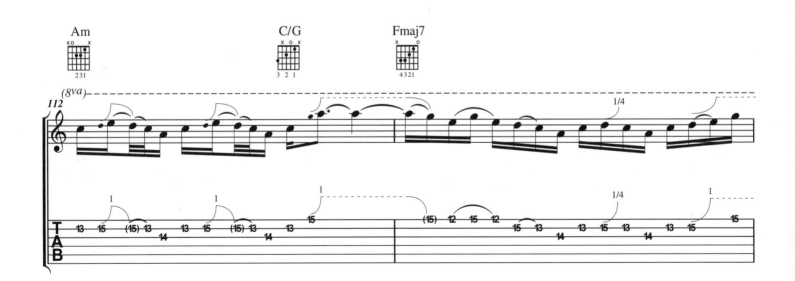

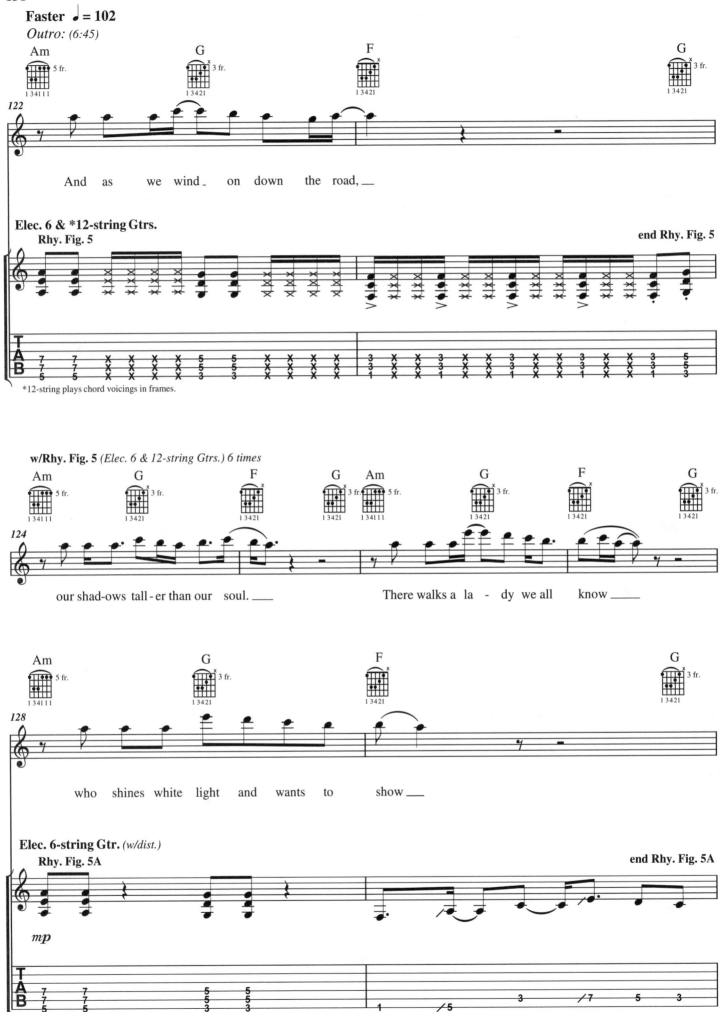

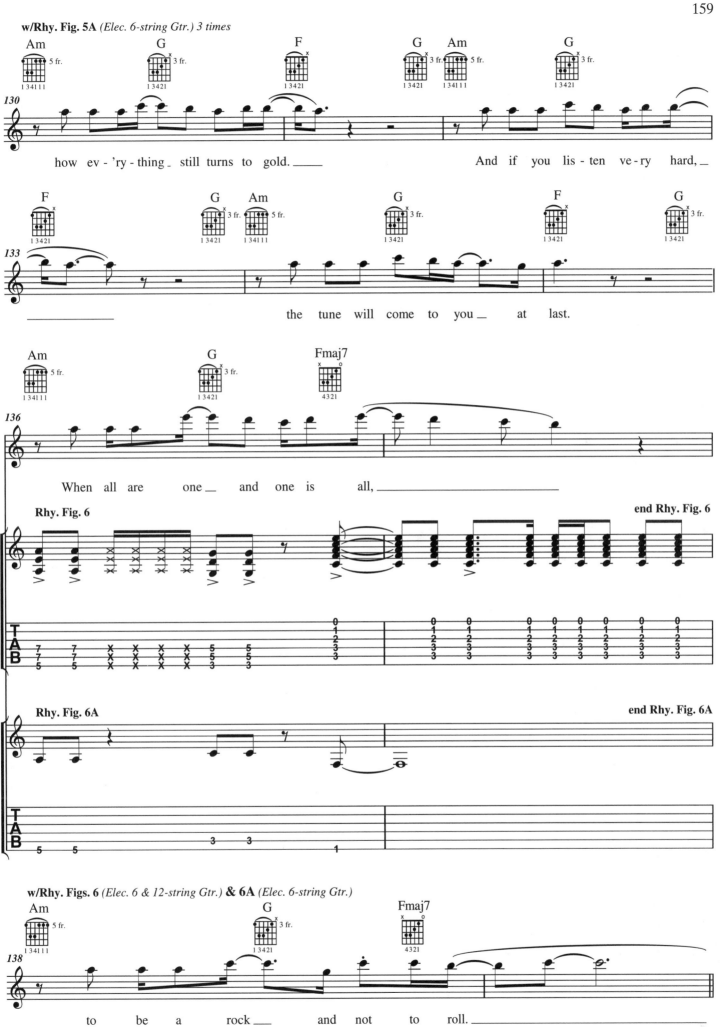

THE SONG REMAINS THE SAME

Words and Music by
JIMMY PAGE and ROBERT PLANT

The Song Remains the Same - 17 - 1

Solo 1:
w/Rhy. Fig. 1 (Gtr. 1) 2 times, simile

Half time ♩ = 72

Verse:

C   G/D   G6/D

I   had   a   dream, __   oh, _____

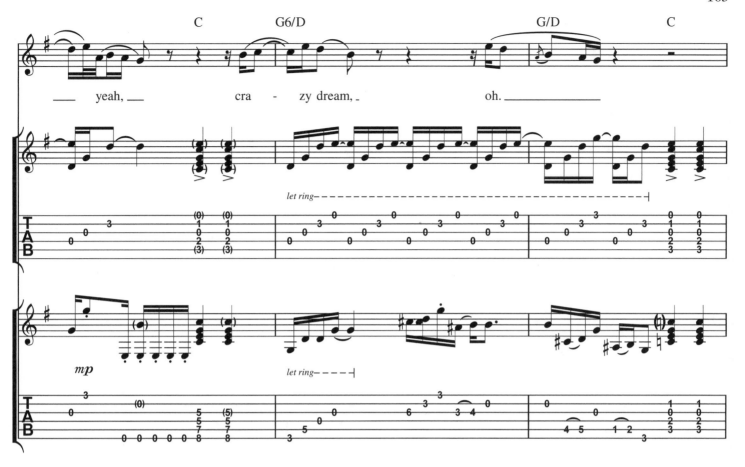

yeah, cra - zy dream, oh.

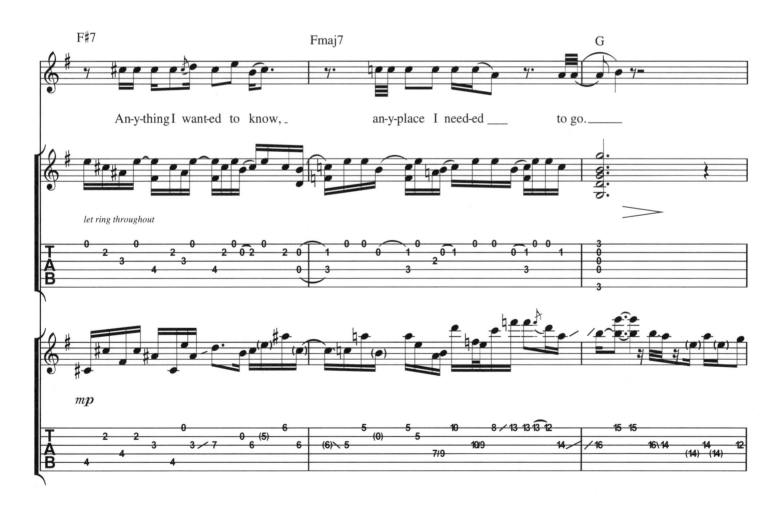

An-y-thing I want-ed to know, an-y-place I need-ed to go.

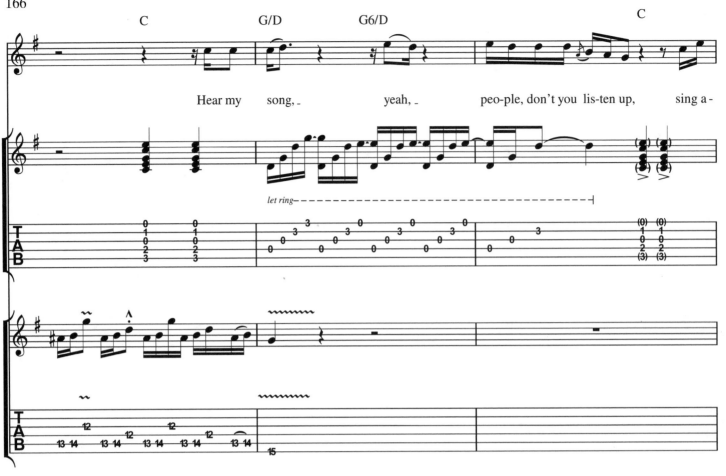

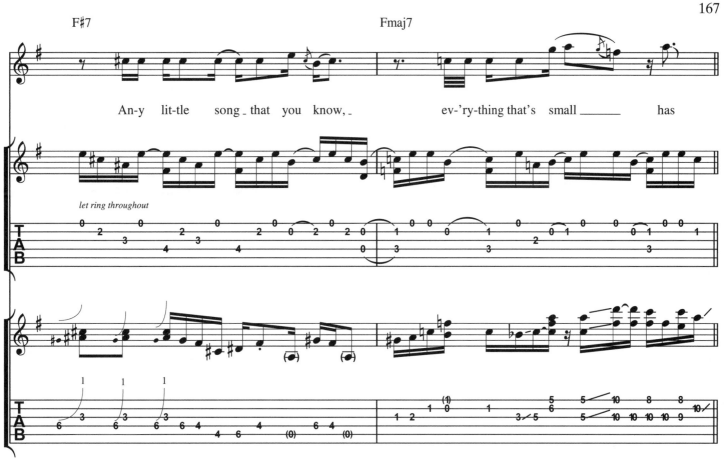

F♯7   **Fmaj7**

An-y lit-tle song that you know, ev-'ry-thing that's small _____ has

let ring throughout

Double time ♩ = 144

G   **A7sus**

to grow. And so it grows. _____ Push, push!

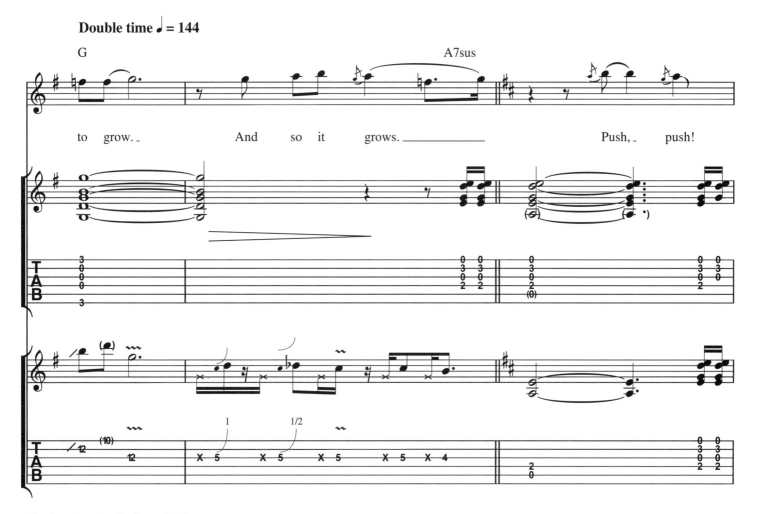

Solo 2:
w/Rhy. Fig. 1, *(Gtr. 1) 2 times, simile*

170

- ing, a, __ slid - ing, a, __ slid - ing, slid-ing, a, slide. _____

Oo, _____

To Coda ⊕

_____ oh, _____ oh, ho. _____

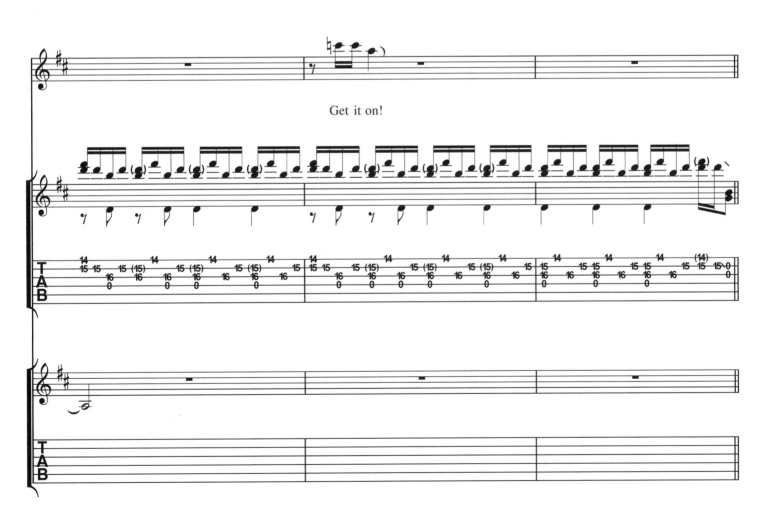

Get it on!

All you got-ta do it now. ___ Ooh _____ me.

D.S. 𝄋 al Coda

Coda

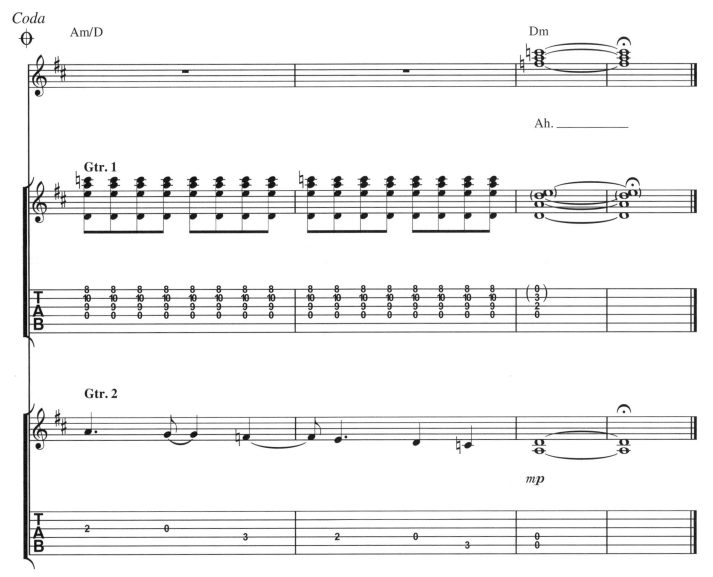

Ah. _____

Gtr. 1

Gtr. 2

mp

OVER THE HILLS AND FAR AWAY

Words and Music by
JIMMY PAGE and ROBERT PLANT

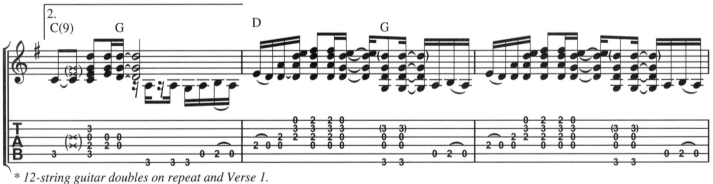

* 12-string guitar doubles on repeat and Verse 1.

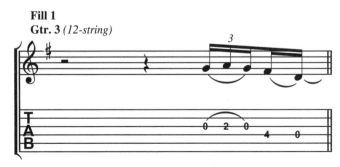

Over the Hills and Far Away - 12 - 1

Verse 1:

so   much, ___   so ___ much. ___

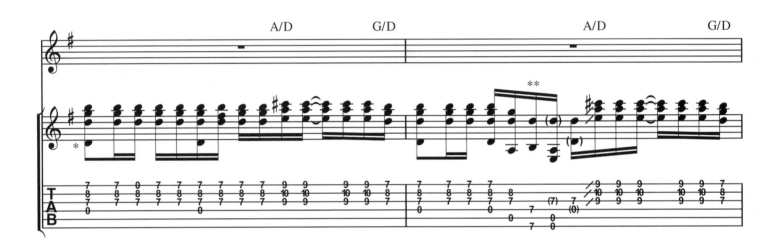

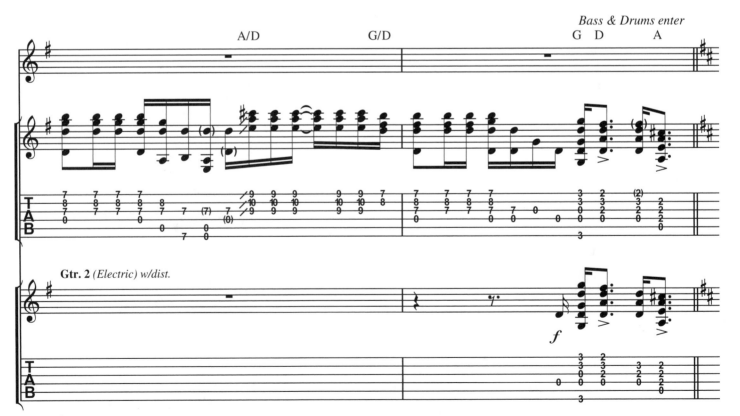

*Let 4th string ring out.
**With thumb.

Over the Hills and Far Away - 12 - 3

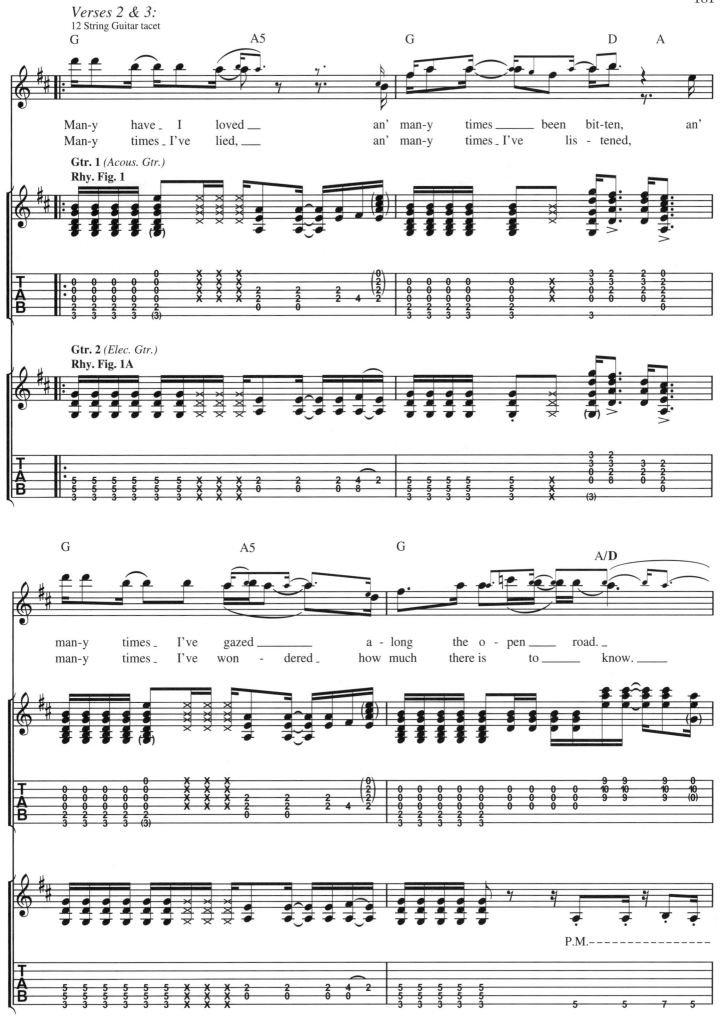

Over the Hills and Far Away - 12 - 5

Verse 4:

184

186

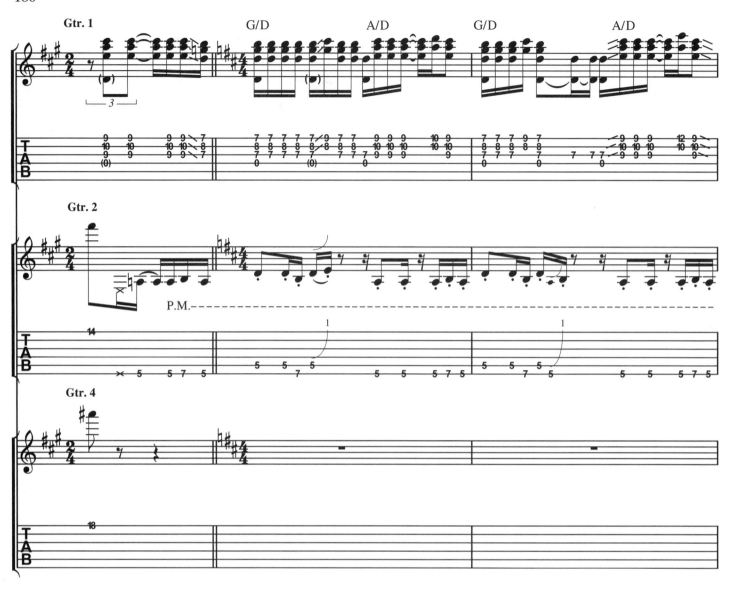

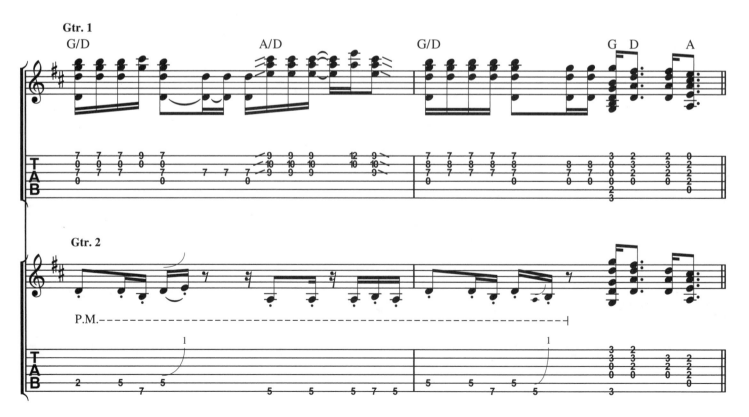

Verse 5:

Mel-low is __ the man __ who knows what he's been miss-in.' Man-y, man - y men __ can't see the o-pen road. _

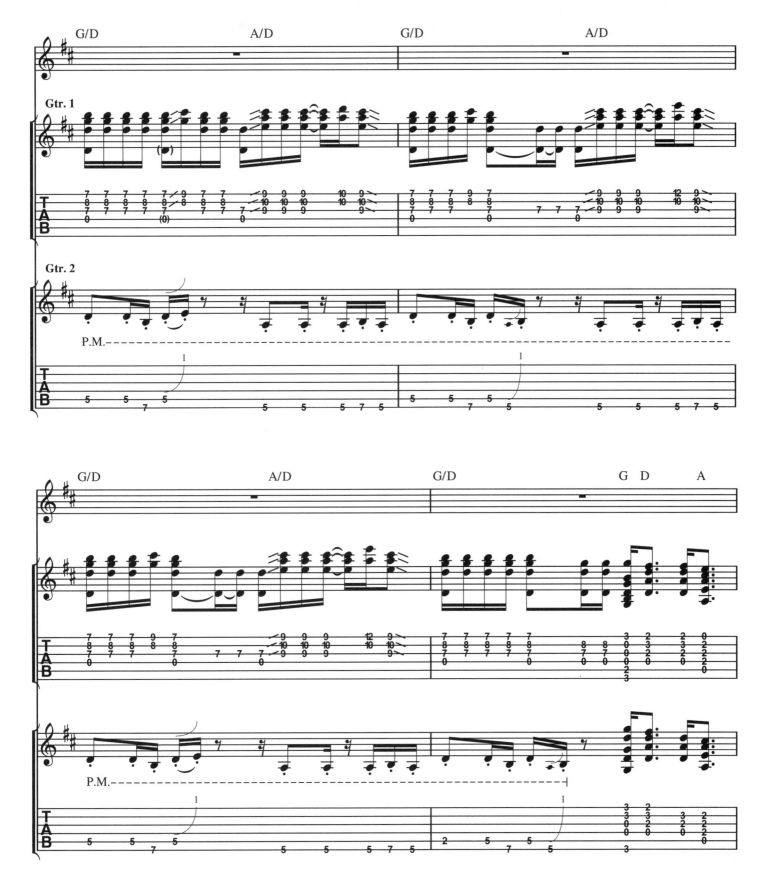

188

Verse 6:

Man-y is — a word — that on - ly leaves you guess-in' a,

guess - in' 'bout a thing — you real - ly ought to know ———— ho, ————

D'YER MAK'ER

Words and Music by
JIMMY PAGE, JOHN BONHAM,
JOHN PAUL JONES and ROBERT PLANT

*Tune down 1/4 tone to play with recording.

D'yer Mak'er - 6 - 1

Verse 5:
w/ Rhy. Fig. 1

Oh, (oh, oh), oh, oh, oh, _ oh, _ oh, _____ you don't have to go. __ Oh, oh, oh, oh, __ you don't have to

go. __ Oh, oh, oh, oh, __ oh, __ ba - by. Babe! Please, please, please _ please! _

Fill 2

Outro Verse:

ah, ah, ah, ah, ah, ba - by. Ah, ah, __ I real-ly love you ba - by.

Palm-mute throughout

Oo, oo, __ oo, __ oo, oo, dar - ling. __ oh, _____

oh, __ ba - by I still love you so. _____

Oh, __ ba - by I still __ love you so. ___ Oh. _____ Oo.

NO QUARTER

Words and Music by
JOHN PAUL JONES , JIMMY PAGE
and ROBERT PLANT

Slowly ♩ = 68

Intro:

C#m7

Elec. Piano *(arr. for gtr.)*

mp   *Let ring throughout*

Theme:
Bass enters

No Quarter - 9 - 1

198

Electric Piano plays simile on repeats
**1st time only*
***Harmonic support by Keyboards. (C# dorian / C# Aeolian)*

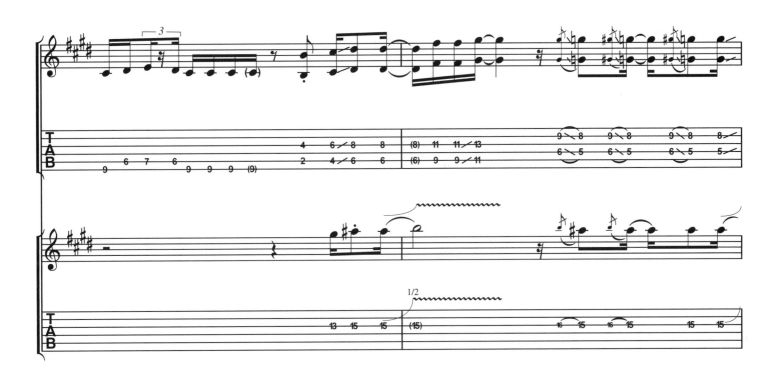

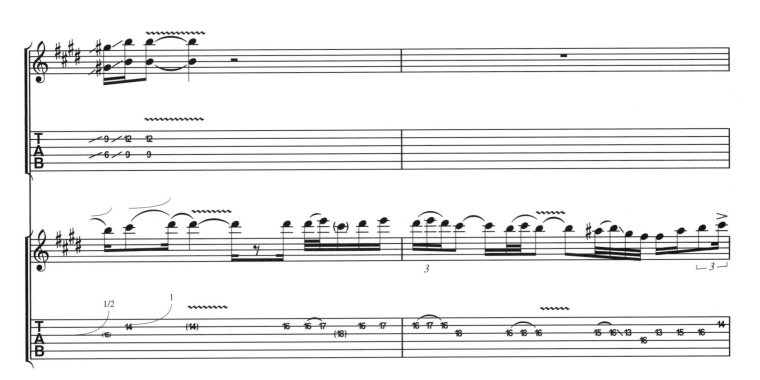

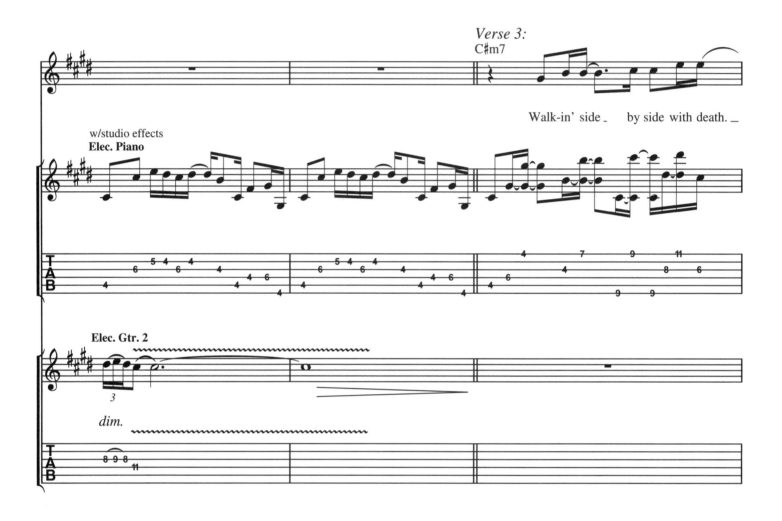

TRAMPLED UNDER FOOT

Words and Music by
JIMMY PAGE, ROBERT PLANT
and JOHN PAUL JONES

Moderately ♩ = 110

Gm

Clavinet

8vb throughout

Verses 1-3:

Gm

1. Greas-y slicked down ̲ bod-y, groov-y leath - er trim, ̲ I like the way you hold ̲ the road.
2.3. *See additional lyrics*

Elec. Gtr. 1
Rhy. Fig. 1

Ma-ma, it ain't ̲ no sin. Talk-in' a-bout love, talk-in' a-bout love, talk-in' a-bout...

end Rhy. Fig. 1

Trampled Under Foot - 10 - 1

Verse 5:
w/Rhy. Fig. 1 (Elec. Gtr. 1)

Fac-t'ry air-con-di - tioned,   heat be-gins _ to rise.   Guar-an-teed to run _ for hours, _

Ma-ma, it's the per-fect size. _   Talk-in' a-bout love,   talk-in' a-bout _ love,   talk-in' a-bout...

Verse 6:
w/Rhy. Fig. 1 *(Elec. Gtr. 1)*

Groov-in' on __ the free-way, gauge is on __ the red. __ Gun down on my gas-o-line, __ be -

lieve I'm gon-na crack your head. __ Talk-in' a-bout _____ love, _____ talk-in' a-bout __

__ love, talk-in' a-bout...

I can't stop talk - in' __ a-bout. I can't stop talk - in' __ a-bout...

Electric Piano Solo:

Elec. Gtr.1

w/wah

Elec. Gtr. 2

w/wah

* Vocal 1st time only

ooh ____ yeah, ____ fine. ____ Drive on!

Elec. Gtrs. 1 & 2 cont. simile

Elec. Gtr. 3

w/wah, reverse reverb & slide

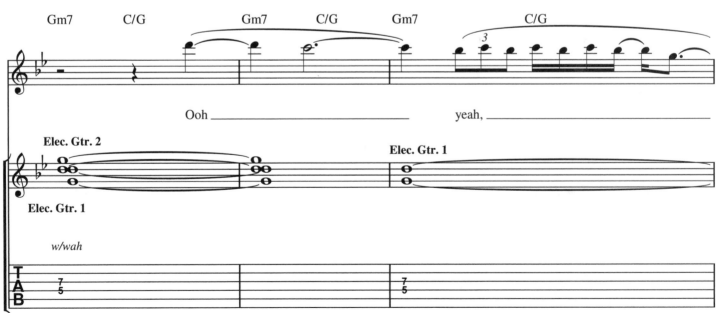

Ooh _____ yeah, _____

Elec. Gtr. 2

Elec. Gtr. 1

Elec. Gtr. 1

w/wah

Gm7   C/G   Gm

___ yes, I'm com-in' through!

Verse 7:
w/ Rhy. Fig. 1 *(Elec. Gtr. 1)*

Come to me ___ for ser - vice ev - 'ry hun - dred miles. Ba - by, let me check ___ your points, ___

Elec. Gtr. 2

w/wah

fix your o - ver-drive. ___ Talk-in'a-bout love, talk-in' a-bout ___ love, talk-in' a-bout...

B♭   C   Gm

Ooh ___ yeah ___

Elec. Gtr. 1

Verse 8:

w/Rhy. Fig. 1 *(Elec. Gtr. 1)*

Gm

Ful-ly *au-to-ma-tic,* comes in an - y size.__ Makes me won-der what I did __ be-

Elec. Gtr.2

fore __ we syn - chro-nized.__ Talk-in' a-bout love, __ talk-in' a - bout __ love, talk-in' a-bout...

Bb   C   Gm

Ooh __

Elec. Gtr. 1

Verse 9:

w/Rhy. Fig. 1 *(Elec. Gtr. 1)*

Gm

Feath - er - light __ sus - pen - sion, coils just could-n't hold. __

Elec. Gtr. 2

Trampled Under Foot - 10 - 8

I'm so glad I took a look in - side your show - room doors, talk-in' a-bout

love, talk-in' a-bout love, talk-in' about...

O - kay O - kay.

Oh!

Verse 2:
Trouble-free transmission helps your oil to flow.
Mama, let me pump your gas, mama, let me do it all.
Talkin' 'bout love...

Verse 3:
Check that heavy metal underneath your hood.
Baby, I could work all night, believe I've got the perfect tools.
Talkin' 'bout love...

HOUSES OF THE HOLY

Words and Music by
JIMMY PAGE and ROBERT PLANT

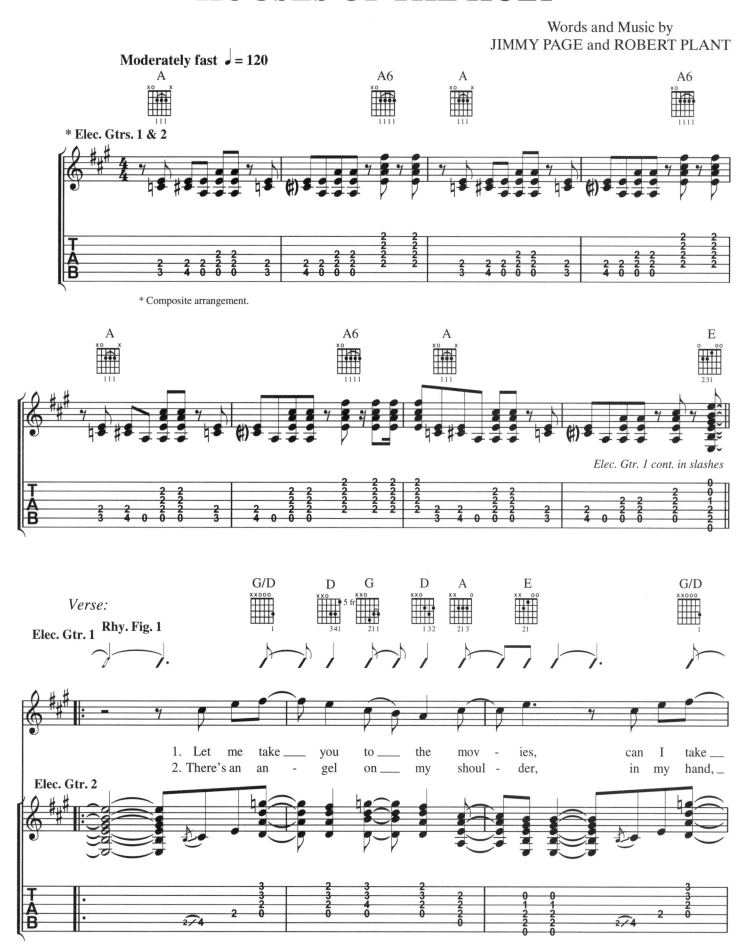

Elec. Gtr. 1 cont. in slashes

Verse:

1. Let me take___ you to___ the mov — ies,   can I take___
2. There's an an — gel on___ my shoul — der,   in my hand,___

Houses of the Holy - 9 - 1

Said there ain't ___ no use ___ in cry -

KASHMIR

Words and Music by
JIMMY PAGE, ROBERT PLANT
and JOHN BONHAM

Guitar Tuning
⑥ = D   ③ = G
⑤ = A   ② = A
④ = D   ① = D

225

Kashmir - 10 - 2

Kashmir - 10 - 4

Ooh, _____ yes, I've been fly - ing. _

My _ ma-ma, ain't no de-ny - ing, _ no de-ny - ing.

Dsus   D   Dm7   Am/D   D5   A/D   Am7/D   G(9)   B♭maj7   Dm

Dsus   D   Dm7   Am/D   D5   A/D   Am7/D   G(9)   B♭maj7   Dm

Oh!

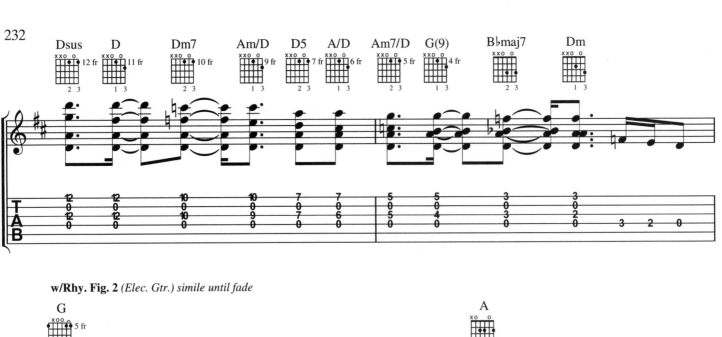

w/Rhy. Fig. 2 *(Elec. Gtr.) simile until fade*

Oh! When I'm on, _ when I'm on _ my way, _ yeah!

When I see, __ when I see the way you stare. _____ Yeah! __

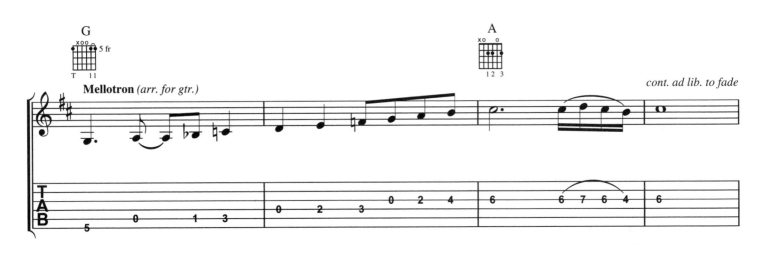

Mellotron *(arr. for gtr.)*

cont. ad lib. to fade

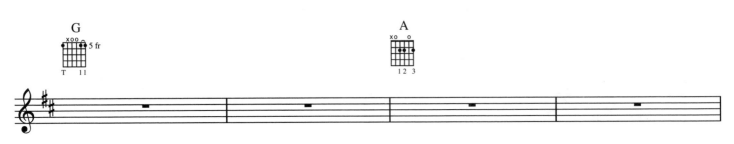

NOBODY'S FAULT BUT MINE

Words and Music by
JIMMY PAGE and ROBERT PLANT

238

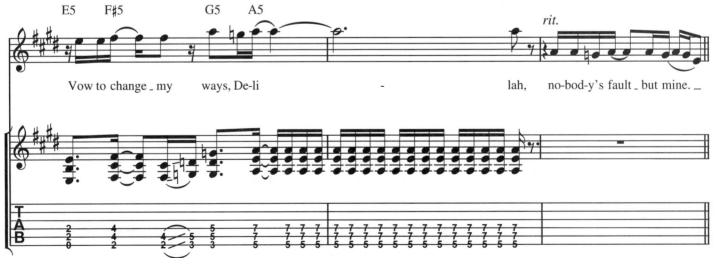

Nobody's Fault but Mine - 14 - 12

ACHILLES LAST STAND

Words and Music by
JIMMY PAGE and ROBERT PLANT

Achilles Last Stand - 30 - 1

It was an Ap-ril morn-in' when they told us we ___ should go, ___

and as I turned to you, you smiled at me, how could we say no? _____

Em
C(9,♯11)
(8va)
4:35
Em
C(9,♯11)
(8va)
Slower (♩ = ♩. = 97)
Gtr. 2
Gtr. 1 (double-tracked)
(Gtr. 1 same as previous 2 bars)
Gtr. 2
Em
D
C
D

oh Al - bi - on re - main (though) sleep - ing now to rise a - gain.

earth.

I'm gon-na reign, gon-na reign, gon-na reign, gon-na reign.

Gtr. 1

Slower ($\bullet$ = $\bullet$. = 97)

Gtr. 1

Gtr. 2

Harmonizer 8va

Gtr. 3

Gtr. 1

tempo (♩ = 146)

Gtr. 1 cont. same as previous two bars.

Where the

might - y arms_ of At - las   hold   the   heav - ens   from_ the   earth. ___

9:04 (E)

Achilles Last Stand - 30 - 28

F#m/E   Em   (E)   D6/E

9:30

Ooh _____

Gtr. 1 *(dbl. tracked)*

F#m/E   Em   (E)   D6/E

F#m(♭6)   Em9

Gtr. 5 *(Elec. 12-Str. Gtr., double tracked with Elec. 12-string Guitar)*

9:43

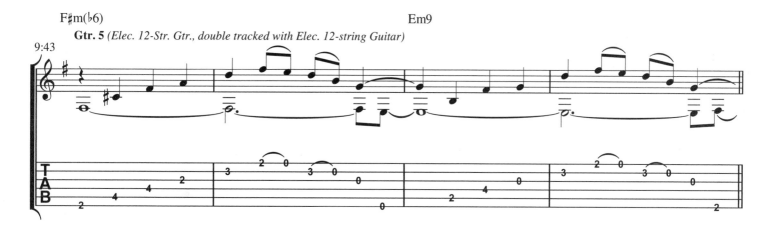

F#m(♭6)   Em9   *Repeat to fade*

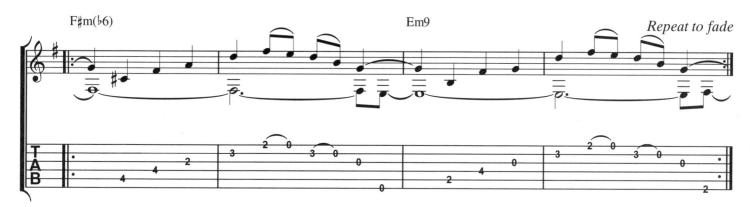

IN THE EVENING

Words and Music by
JOHN PAUL JONES, JIMMY PAGE
and ROBERT PLANT

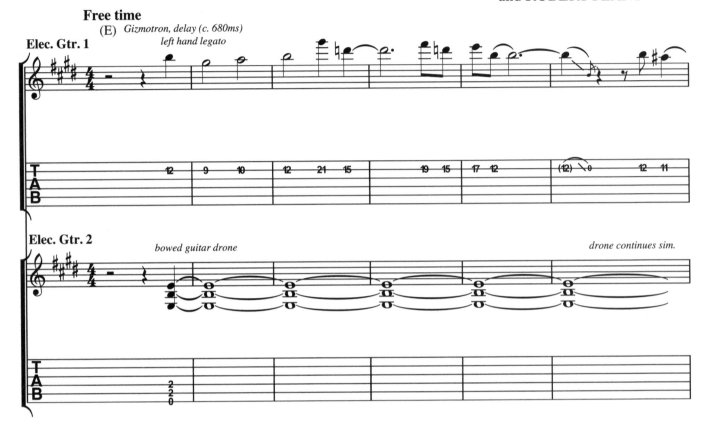

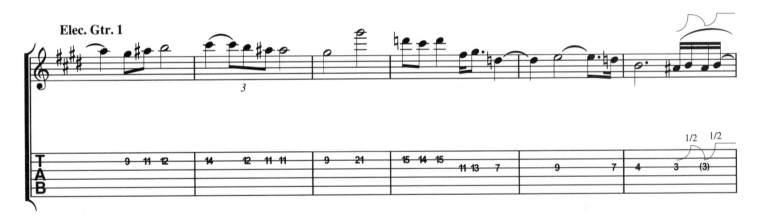

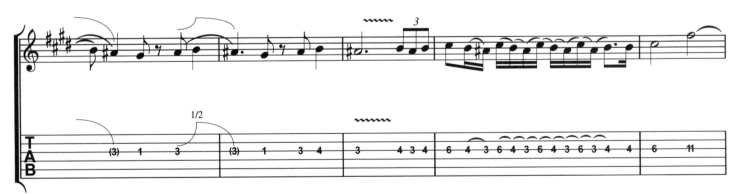

In the Evening - 11 - 1

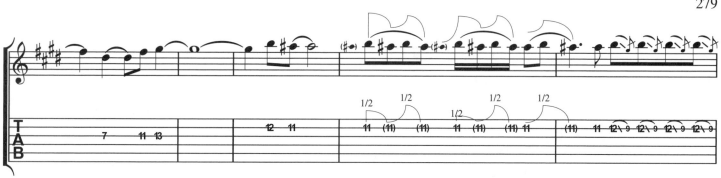

In the eve - ning

drone ends

Verse 1:
a tempo ♩ = 104

when the day is done, —

Rhy. Fig. 1

P.M.

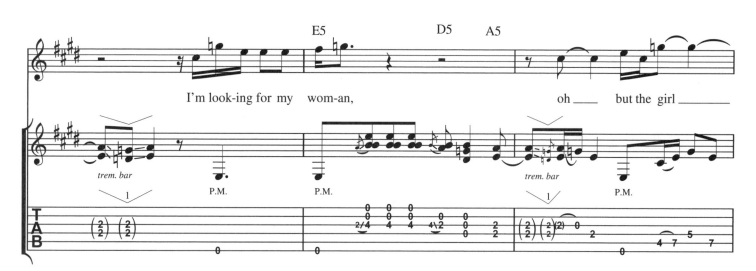

I'm look-ing for my wom-an,

oh ___ but the girl ___

trem. bar   P.M.   P.M.   *trem. bar*   P.M.

In the Evening - 11 - 8

*Chord names denote overall harmony.

4. Ooh _____ what -

ALL MY LOVE

Words and Music by
JOHN PAUL JONES and ROBERT PLANT

All My Love - 9 - 1

294

All My Love - 9 - 6

All My Love - 9 - 7

GUITAR TAB GLOSSARY

TABLATURE EXPLANATION

TAB illustrates the six strings of the guitar.
Notes and chords are indicated by the placement of fret numbers on each string.

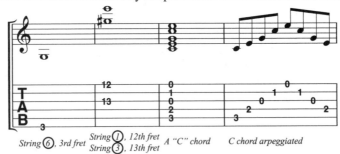

String ⑥, 3rd fret   *String ①, 12th fret*   *A "C" chord*   *C chord arpeggiated*
                       String ③, 13th fret

BENDING NOTES

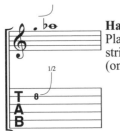

Half Step:
Play the note and bend string one half step (one fret).

Whole Step:
Play the note and bend string one whole step (two frets).

Slight Bend/ Quarter-Tone Bend:
Play the note and bend string sharp.

Prebend (Ghost Bend):
Bend to the specified note before the string is plucked.

Prebend and Release:
Play the already-bent string, then immediately drop it down to the fretted note.

Unison Bend:
Play both notes and immediately bend the lower note to the same pitch as the higher note.

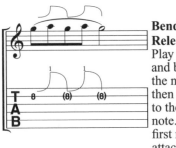

Bend and Release:
Play the note and bend to the next pitch, then release to the original note. Only the first note is attacked.

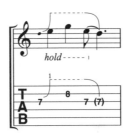

Bends Involving More Than One String:
Play the note and bend the string while playing an additional note on another string. Upon release, relieve the pressure from the additional note allowing the original note to sound alone.

Bends Involving Stationary Notes:
Play both notes and immediately bend the lower note up to pitch. Release bend as indicated.

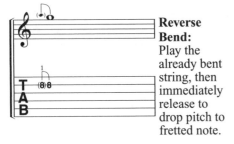

Reverse Bend:
Play the already bent string, then immediately release to drop pitch to fretted note.

Unison Bend:
Play both notes and immediately bend the lower note to the same pitch as the higher note.

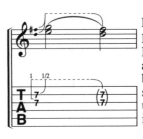

Double Note Bend:
Play both notes and immediately bend both strings simultaneously up the indicated intervals.

ARTICULATIONS

 **Hammer On (Ascending Slur):** Play the lower note, then "hammer" your finger to the higher note. Only the first note is plucked.

 **Pull Off (Descending Slur):** Play the higher note with your first finger already in position on the lower note. Pull your finger off the first note with a strong downward motion that plucks the string—sounding the lower note.

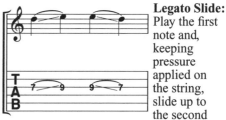 **Legato Slide:** Play the first note and, keeping pressure applied on the string, slide up to the second note. The diagonal line shows that it is a slide and not a hammer-on or a pull-off.

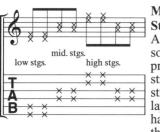 **Muted Strings:** A percussive sound is produced by striking the strings while laying the fret hand across them.

 **Palm Mute:** The notes are muted (muffled) by placing the palm of the pick hand lightly on the strings, just in front of the bridge.

 **Left Hand Hammer:** Using only the left hand, hammer on the first note played on each string.

 **Glissando:** Play note and slide in specified direction.

 **Bend and Tap Technique:** Play note and bend to specified interval. While holding bend, tap onto fret indicated with a "t."

 **Fretboard Tapping:** Tap onto the note indicated by the "t" with a finger of the pick hand, then pull off to the following note held by the fret hand.

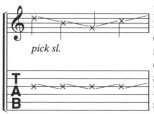 **Pick Slide:** Slide the edge of the pick in specified direction across the length of the strings.

 **Tremolo Picking:** The note or notes are picked as fast as possible.

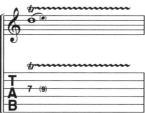 **Trill:** Hammer on and pull off consecutively and as fast as possible between the original note and the grace note.

 **Vibrato:** The pitch of a note is varied by a rapid shaking of the fret-hand finger, wrist, and forearm.

 **Accent:** Notes or chords are to be played with added emphasis.

 **Staccato (Detached Notes):** Notes or chords are to be played about half their noted value and with separation.

HARMONICS

Natural Harmonic:
A finger of the fret hand lightly touches the string at the note indicated in the TAB and is plucked by the pick producing a bell-like sound called a harmonic.

Artificial Harmonic:
Fret the note at the first TAB number, lightly touch the string at the fret indicated in parens (usually 12 frets higher than the fretted note), then pluck the string with an available finger or your pick.

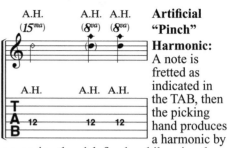

Artificial "Pinch" Harmonic:
A note is fretted as indicated in the TAB, then the picking hand produces a harmonic by squeezing the pick firmly while using the tip of the index finger in the pick attack. If parenthesis are found around the fretted note, it does not sound. No parenthesis means both the fretted note and the A.H. are heard simultaneously.

RHYTHM SLASHES

Strum Marks/ Rhythm Slashes:
Strum with the indicated rhythm pattern. Strum marks can be located above the staff or within the staff.

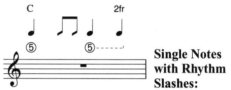

Single Notes with Rhythm Slashes:
Sometimes single notes are incorporated into a strum pattern. The circled number below is the string and the fret number is above.

TREMOLO BAR

Specified Interval:
The pitch of a note or chord is lowered to the specified interval and then return as indicated. The action of the tremolo bar is graphically represented by the peaks and valleys of the diagram.

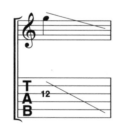

Unspecified Interval:
The pitch of a note or chord is lowered, usually very dramatically, until the pitch of the string becomes indeterminate.

PICK DIRECTION

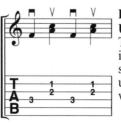

Downstrokes and Upstrokes:
The downstroke is indicated with this symbol (⊓) and the upstroke is indicated with this (∨).